In our prim, prudish, and restrictive past, the jokes collected in this book would not have been told in mixed company; they might even have made grown men blush.

Welcome to the 1980s where these racy tales have been taken out of the locker room and into the full light of day, to be enjoyed without restraint.

This book does not mince words. It will provide hours of genial fun and side-splitting laughter.

Just one word of caution: unless your grandma is a real swinger, keep this book out of her hands.

DIRTY STORIES

for all occasions

ANDREW L. CLEVELAND

Galahad Books • New York City

Published in 1980 by
Galahad Books
95 Madison Avenue
New York, New York 10016

Library of Congress Catalog Card Number: 79-52809

ISBN: 0-88365-442-3

Printed in the United States of America

DIRTY STORIES
for all occasions

A STATELY LADY VISITED the zoo, and stared at the animals with great interest. Quite non-plussed, she pored over the signs in two adjacent cages and then asked the keeper, "Pray, sir, what is the difference between the American porcupine and the European porcupine? They look much the same to me!"

"Well" answered the attendant, "there's really no difference at all except that the prick of the European porcupine is nine inches long, while that of the American porcupine is only seven."

Highly indignant, the lady trotted off in a huff to the curator's office. She demanded that the attendant be discharged.

"Oh!" the curator explained, "You misunderstood him. What he meant to convey was that the quill of the European porcupine is nine inches long, while the quill of the American porcupine is only seven inches long. As a matter of fact, neither one's prick is more than two inches long."

A Parisian impressario, announced that a sensational show would be shown in a Montmartre hall. He would produce an incredible young man who would screw 10—yes, 10 women—in one hour.

The hall was packed. All tickets had been sold. On the stage, were 10 beds side by side, with a pretty girl on each one of them.

The young man stepped forth to great applause, flexed his muscles, and then sprang into the first bed. It took him but two minutes to do the job, and then he leaped into the second bed.

He did his thing, and then went to the third bed. The audience was rapt in attention. Then the incredible man serviced the fourth damsel, then with but a minutes' rest, the fifth. The hall rocked with applause. Then the sixth girl.

But when he got to the seventh, he could proceed no further. The audience felt bilked. The hall was filled with catcalls, and loud irate demands for refunds.

The producer was beside himself. He approached the performer. "Mon Dieu! You have ruined me!"

"I cannot understand it," the performer answered, "only an hour ago, in rehearsal, I was perfect!"

Man Cannot Live on Bread Alone

A soldier had just come back from duty. He had a two-day pass. As he stepped off the train, his girl friend met him, and threw her arms around him.

They were walking down the platform, chatting amiably, when all of a sudden they broke into a loud argument. The shouting between them became so intense that soon a crowd formed.

Finally a man stepped up to the soldier, and inquired, "Say, buddy, what's going on? What's the matter?"

Instead of answering, the soldier kept shouting to his girl, "F. F.," while she kept shouting back, "E. F."

"What's E. F.?" asked the peacemaker.

The soldier replied, "She wants to eat first."

A Bird in the Hat Is Worth . . .

Pat and Mike were walking down the street. Said Pat, "Mike, I've got awful cramps. If I don't take a shit right this minute, I'll pass out!"

"Okay," said Mike, "I'll stand a bit down the street and lay chickie. If anyone comes, I'll let you know."

Pat squatted and relieved himself. Then out of nowhere, Clancy the cop came parading down the street. Mike yelled, "Pat, here comes Clancy, and he's coming right toward us."

"Uh," cried Mike, pulling up his pants, "we'll have to do something quick." In a flash, he took off his hat and dropped it over the evidence.

Up came Clancy, and eyed the two suspiciously. "And what have you got there under that hat?" the cop asked.

"Oh," said Mike, "we just caught a bird."

"Ah-hah," said Clancy, "a bird, is it? And you've got it under the hat?"

Yes," said Pat, "that's where it is."

"Okay," offered Clancy helpfully, "you lift the hat very slowly, and I'll make a grab for it."

JOHNSON DIED. The moment after his death, he found himself before St. Peter who consigned him to Hell.

An angel brought him down to show him his new habitation. Immediately upon entering, Johnson was surprised to see before him a well-dressed gentleman sitting relaxed, sipping a glass of champagne. He held the glass with his right hand, and with his left he circled the waist of a gorgeous girl, dressed in a seductive chiffon negligee.

"Oh!" said Johnson, "This is Hell? What a wonderful place!"

"Ah!" answered the angel. "Things are not what they seem. The glass the man is holding has a hole in it; the girl hasn't."

A LADY HAD A LARGE "W" tattoed on her right buttock. She also had another large "W" tattoed on her left buttock. And when she bent over—W O W!

Pulling Rank

The blonde came to the doctor's office complaining she felt a burning sensation when she went to the bathroom.

"You've got P.D.," said the doctor.

"What's that?" she asked.

"Why, that's a private disease," answered the physician.

"That faker!" shouted the blonde. "He told me he was a lieutenant."

WHAT'S THE DIFFERENCE between a vitamin and a hormone?

You can't hear a vitamin.

The duke woke up in a very manly condition. He summoned Jeeves.

"Ah," said Jeeves, when he saw what he hadn't seen in months. "Shall I summon the Duchess?"

"Oh, no!" said the Duke, "Just fetch me a pair of very baggy trousers. I'm going to try to smuggle this thing into London."

A LADY VISITED the zoo with her young daughter. She brought the little girl before the enclosure which held the elephants. The little girl turned to her mother and said, "Mother, what is that big thing the elephant has sticking out from his face?"

The mother answered, "Oh, that's the elephant's trunk. He picks up things with it, and he smells with it."

The little girl continued, "And mother, what is that long thing between the elephant's legs?"

"Oh," answered the mother, "that's the elephant's tail."

"No, no," said the little girl, "there's something else. There's something else that's sticking out between the elephant's legs."

The embarrassed mother answered, "Oh, that's nothing! That's nothing at all!"

A Frenchman standing by overheard the answer. Turning toward the mother, he blandly remarked, "Ah, I see! Madam is blasé!"

Service with a Smile

The debutante daughter of a wealthy family went off to a party and came home smashing drunk. She could hardly get herself up the stairs; the butler had to assist her. However, when he got her into her bedroom, she was so ossified that she couldn't get under the bedsheets, and he had to undress her and put her to bed.

The next morning, she had some dim recollection of the state she had been in, and the circumstances of the homecoming. She called the butler and said, "James, I don't remember much about last night except that you tried to give me some coffee which I couldn't down and that I couldn't get up the stairs. How did I come to wake up in bed?"

"Well," he answered, "you came home very tired, my lady."

But she pressed on. "James, I'm undressed and I'm in my nightgown."

"Well, I couldn't let you spoil your good evening clothes, my lady."

"Oh," she stammered, "do you mean that you undressed me and put me to bed without my knowing it? Tell the truth, was I tight?"

"Yes, my lady; but not after the first time."

IF ALL THE FRESHMEN at Yale were laid end to end—no one would be surprised.

A VISITOR FROM BOSTON got off at Grand Central Station in New York and jumped into a cab. It was 10 o'clock at night and the visitor hadn't eaten his supper. He was rather hungry.

The Bostonian was particularly fond of fish. He leaned toward the cabbie and said, "Tell me, mister, do you know where I can get scrod at this time of night?"

The cabbie scratched his head for a moment and answered, "You know, sir, in my 20 years in the taxi business, I've been asked that question over a thousand times; but I must tell you that this is the first time in all my experience that anybody has phrased that query in the past pluperfect."

WHAT DO THEY CALL Ex-Lax in Holland?

Dutch Cleanser.

Tanked Up for Tiger

It happened in Africa. A political rebel had been condemned to death. However, the Sultan was in an indulgent frame of mind. When the prisoner was brought before him, his Majesty declared: "I'm going to give you a chance for your life. Before us, there stand three tents. In each tent, there is an almost superhuman task to perform. If you succeed in all three tents, I'll pardon you.

"In the first tent is a gallon of wine: you must drink it all down within 15 minutes.

"In the second tent is a ferocious tiger, suffering from a horrible toothache. You must extract the tooth in 15 minutes.

"In the third tent, there is a powerfully built Amazonian virgin, who has resisted the advances of the strongest men in my realm. You cannot overpower her, but you have 15 minutes to seduce her."

The prisoner thanked the Sultan for being given a chance to live, and then proceeded to the first tent.

In 10 minutes, he emerged staggeringly drunk, holding upside-down an empty wine jug in one hand. On unsteady feet, he plunged into the second tent.

Seconds later, everyone's blood curdled because of the terrible screams and roars which came forth from that tent. About eight minutes later, the prisoner emerged from the second tent, a horrible bloody mess, covered with long scratches, deep bites, and fearful gouges from the tiger's claws. To look at him was sickening.

Reeling up to one of the royal attendants, the prisoner demanded: "Now where's the girl with the toothache?"

Look, Ma, No Hands!

A man, who had neither arms nor legs approached the door of a house of ill fame.

The madam emerged, took one look at him, and said, "Say mister! I'm dreadfully sorry! But how can you possibly do business here?"

"How can I do business?" he retorted. "How do you think I rang the bell?"

Panadian Holiday

A business man was on holiday in Canada. He decided to take advantage of the fine lake at his camp, so he wired his secretary in Rochester: "Send up two punts and a canoe."

His dutiful secretary wired back: "The girls are on their way, but what the hell is a 'panoe'?"

BUSINESS WAS LOUSY. Morris Ginsberg of Ginsberg's Catskill Resort was just about ready to give up the hotel business and try something new.

"But," as he told his niece, who was visiting him during her college vacation, "at my age it's not easy to get started again."

"Uncle Morris, there's nothing wrong with the hotel . . . except that you don't have customers. What you need is a gimmick to bring them in."

"A gimmick," he echoed, "maybe you're right. But what kind of gimmick?"

So they put their heads together and decided on a Wild West motif. Ginsberg spent the last of his savings redecorating the hotel to look like one he'd seen in a cowboy picture. To go with the new look, he renamed the hotel "Westward-Ho." The crowning glory was a stagecoach which he bought cheap from his cousin, the movie producer.

When everything was all ready he told his black driver, Franklin, to ride the stagecoach down to the train station to look for prospective guests. "If we offer them a free ride to the Westward-Ho—in a stagecoach no less—we're sure to attract customers!"

Franklin returned hours later with a stagecoach full of men. Ginsberg knew his luck had changed. Everytime a train came in, Franklin was there to meet it; and everytime he came back he brought dozens of customers. But all males!

Ginsberg was full of praise for his driver. "Franklin," he said, "I'm giving you a raise. What do you do that brings those men into our hotel?"

"Mr. Ginsberg," replied Franklin, "Ah didn't do nuthin' special. Ah jest pointed to dat stagecoach and yelled 'Dis way to de Westward-Ho House!'"

A YOUNG LAD had a pernicious habit of betting. His father consulted with his schoolteacher as to how he might be cured.

The schoolteacher said, "Well, he's got to lose one big bet. The loss must hurt him. That's the only way to cure him." The father agreed.

The next day, the kid came to class as usual. After the day was over and everybody had gone, he stalked up to the teacher and impudently declared, "You give everybody the impression that you're a natural blonde; but the fact is, you're cheating. I know that you dye your hair."

"What!" she exclaimed in fury. "You insulting brat!"

"Yes! You're sore because I know the truth," he exclaimed. "I'll bet you $25 that you dye your hair. $25! Do you know what that kind of money means to me? That's five weeks' pocket money, but I'll put $25 on the line to make my point. You're not a blonde, you're a brunette! And you use dye on your hair to deceive everyone."

Furious, she replied, "I'll take your bet, you little scoundrel!"

"Well," he replied, "there's only one way to prove it. You pick up your skirt and show me the hair on your pussy. If it's black, then I win; and if it's blonde, you win."

Cornered, she had little choice. Everybody had gone, and they were alone. She had made a promise to his father to cure him, and she was going to. So she lifted up her skirt and exposed herself. As she picked up the money, she said, "You miserable imp! That'll teach you not to bet."

When the boy had gone, she called up his father and told him the story. She said, "Now he's lost $25. He'll be cured."

"Hell and damnation!" cried his father, "Only this morning he bet me $50 he'd see your cunt before the day was out."

Nuptial Athlete

They were on their honeymoon. The bride was so nervous in the bedroom that the glass of water in her hand trembled. It was very unfortunate, for the groom slipped on the floor, and pole-vaulted out the window.

A MAN CAME INTO the dentist's office, and immediately requested the nurse leave the room. The dentist sent her out. Then the patient unzipped his fly and took out his pecker.

The dentist said, "Look mister, you're in the wrong place. I don't treat clap. Why don't you go to an M.D.?"

"No, no!" answered the other. "You're the man I want to see. There's a tooth embedded in it."

The Duchess of Marlboro was visiting a wounded captain at a military hospital. He had been accidentally shot in target practice.

The Duchess asked the officer, "Sir, just where were you wounded?"

The captain squirmed for a moment and then said, "I'm sorry, Madam, but I'd rather not discuss this delicate matter."

"Tut-tut," said the Duchess, "I've been married now for 15 years."

Not wanting to be rude, the captain replied, "I was shot in the penis."

The Duchess continued, "Was the bone broken?"

The officer sat bolt upright in bed, bowed slightly and remarked, "Fifteen years married, you say. Duchess, my compliments to the Duke."

Rugby:

A game played by men with peculiarly shaped balls.

An expert on the subject of wines and liquors was asked, "What is the correct number of drinks a person should have at one meal?"

His answer: "Drinks are like tits. One isn't enough, and three are too many."

A WOMAN, WHO HAD BEEN browsing around in a furniture store for an hour or so, finally decided to buy a certain bed, and asked the salesman, who had been following in her wake, to write up the order. But while he was writing it, she changed her mind, and decided to cancel the order.

Much embarrassed to tell the salesman who had spent so much time with her, she blurted out: "Sorry, I'm not going to take the bed. I think I'd rather have an occasional piece in the living room."

WHAT HAS FOUR LEGS and flies?

Two pairs of pants.

Love Is Blind

A young Frenchman and a girl he was crazy about were driving down the Champs Elysees. He was fondling her; and she, in a paroxysm of frenzy, had unbuttoned his fly and was rubbing his dick.

He just couldn't stand the tension any longer, so he said to her, "Look, honey, I can't wait till we get to the Bois de Boulogne. I must do it right away. Let's stop the car here, and we'll get out, and we'll get under. We'll make believe we're fixing the engine." She agreed.

About 30 minutes later, the young man was tapped on the shoulder by a gendarme who stood over him.

"My dear young man," said the officer, "I do not disturb you because you have blocked traffic a full two miles down the boulevard. No, not for that. Nor do I disturb you because you have caused a crowd of 3,000 people to gather here at this spot. No, not for that. But as an officer of the law, it is my duty to inform you that your car has been stolen."

A PARSON SAUNTERED INTO his golf club one weekday morning. He wanted to play a round of golf, but nobody familiar was in sight. The only other person in the locker room was a stranger.

The parson approached him and said, "Are you looking for a game?"

"Yes. I'd be glad to play with you. But I always play for $10.00 a round."

The parson realized he wasn't much of a golfer, but he was willing to pay $10.00 for the morning's pleasure and exercise, so he agreed.

Out on the links, the stranger took every unfair advantage. When the parson was putting, he'd start to jabber away. He cheated whenever he could, and he made the day miserable.

After the parson had paid off, he turned to the stranger and said, "Here's my card. Come to my church any Sunday. I'll be glad to see you, and give you my greetings. And you might bring along your parents, too. I'd like to meet them."

"Bring along my father and mother? Why?"

"Because then," rejoined the parson, "I could marry them."

A LADY OF LEISURE stopped at a little town in the West. Her calling soon became known, and she received visits from the town's male population, young and old, married and single. So keen was the ardor of her admirers that they visited her again and again. In fact, she completely captivated the town.

Finally, the elders of the church met and determined to put a stop to the young woman's operations. The chief of police was on his vacation and the mayor would not act in the matter, so action devolved on the churchmen themselves. A committee of three called on the girl.

"We must approach her gently," said the deacon, "and persuade her to leave without a scandal." When they got to her house, he again said, "Let us not alarm her by a show of force.

You, gentlemen, wait down here, and I'll go up and speak to her."

But the moments turned into minutes, and the minutes turned into an hour, and still the deacon had not come down.

The two who waited for him began to grumble. After another half-hour, down came the deacon. "There is nothing for us to do here," he said, shaking his head, "this young woman has been grossly maligned. In the short talk I had with her, I found her to be a most cultured girl. We have no right to force her to leave town."

"All right," replied one of the others wearily, "button up your pants and let's go!"

DON'T PISS ON THE FLOOR—the next man may have holes in his shoes.

Three Gay Blades

An American sojourning in Paris had made friends with a young Frenchman. One night, the Frenchman called him and said, "Tom, get out of bed, quick! Come here, quick! Quick!"

They looked across the street and there were three French fairies involved in an orgy. All three were standing up—one next to each other—and each was completely nude, and all were pumping away.

"Ah," exclaimed the Frenchman, "Lucky Jacques! He's in the middle."

FIRST MORON: It's very nice out tonight.
SECOND MORON: Yes. I think I'll take mine out, too.

Exotica

In an anthropological institute in Vienna, there used to be great interest in the various love postures of the races. Two professors, one a Frenchman and the other a German, devoted most of their waking hours to the matter, consulting such ancient texts as the *Kama Sutra* and the *Perfumed Garden*. When they finally conferred to compare notes, they disagreed on only one point: the German said there were 138 postures: the Frenchman claimed there were 139.

A hot argument ensued. It was decided to enumerate the positions. "Well," the Frenchman began, "first, of course, there's the good old way."

"Ach!" exlaimed the German professor, disgustedly. "You win! I forgot about that one!"

Cutting Him Down to Size

A young lady was querying her analyst about some of the sexual terms used in Freudian literature.

"What's a phallic symbol?" she asked.

"A phallic symbol," explained the doctor, "represents a phallus."

"And what is a phallus?" persisted the girl.

"Well," the psychiatrist said, "the best way I can explain that is to show you." And he stood up, unzipped his fly, and took out his pecker. "This, Miss Burns, is a phallus."

"Oh," said the girl, "I understand. You mean it's like a prick, only smaller."

THE TOWN WAS IN an uproar. An inmate of the local lunatic asylum had escaped and had raped two women. Everybody was horrified.

Late that afternoon, the local newspaper's headline ran: NUT BOLTS AND SCREWS.

A MAN STRODE INTO a fish store and said, "Tell me, how much are crabs today?"

"Seventy cents apiece," the fishmonger answered.

The customer thrust out his right hand and exclaimed: "Shake hands with a millionaire!"

PSYCHOLOGIST: Do you cheat on your wife?
PATIENT: Who else?

Gotcha!

The golf pro came into the clubhouse, and was introduced to a new member. The new member said he'd like a game, but that he didn't shoot very well. The pro thought he would be an easy mark and said that his usual stakes for playing with anybody were $50 a match.

The new member replied that he hadn't any objection to the amount of the wager, but that since he was a very poor player he required a handicap.

"What handicap do you want?" said the pro. "I'll give you five holes."

"No," said the newcomer. "I don't want five holes, I just want two gotchas."

"Gotchas?" asked the pro. "What the hell are gotchas? I've heard of mulligans, and have heard of all kinds of other handicaps, but I've never heard of gotchas."

"Well," said the newcomer, "if you want to play me for $50, that's what I want—two gotchas. I'll explain to you as we go on what gotchas are."

"O.K.," said the pro, believing that he could hardly lose to a dub like this one. The most he'd have to forfeit would be two holes.

So they proceeded to the links. The pro won the first four holes with ease. On the fifth hole—a par three—the newcomer hit his ball straight onto the green, and the ball trickled to within five inches of the pin. The pro also landed on the green, but his ball was seven feet away from the pin, a more or less routine putt for a club pro.

First, the pro lined up his ball carefully, then he examined the turf, then he bent over his ball with his putter. But just as he began to stroke the ball, the newcomer stole up behind him, and grabbed his testicles, and cried, "Gotcha."

Of course, the pro missed the putt. The dub won the hole, and the score was now 4 to 1.

About two hours later, both players came back to the clubhouse. The pro was asked by an old member how he made out with the newcomer. "I lost," he said, shamefacedly.

"You lost?" cried the other, incredulously. "How could you lose to that guy? He can't possibly get around the course in under 90!"

"Yes, I know," said the pro. "I should have taken him easily. But have you ever tried swinging at a golf ball while waiting for a second gotcha?"

Tight Spot

Mrs. McCarthy moved to a new apartment in which there were new plumbing facilities. Elated at the sight of the bathroom, she plumped herself down hard on the seat only to find ten minutes later that she couldn't extricate herself.

In panic, she called Mr. McCarthy who tried to pull her out, but couldn't budge her.

"Well," said McCarthy, "there's nothing for it, but I'll have to call the plumber."

And for modesty's sake, he took his top hat out of the closet, and placed it over Mrs. McCarthy's pubic region. "It would be a slander and a shame," he murmered, "to let the plumber come and see Mrs. McCarthy in a state of sheer nakedness."

In short time, Scanlon, the plumber, made an appearance. He took a hold of Mrs. McCarthy's hand, and pulled and pulled, but he couldn't wrench her out of the seat.

He then turned to McCarthy and said, "Mr. McCarthy, I can chisel the seat away and save *her*, but the man's a goner!"

FOR YEARS, Jakie had been urging to have a little kooky sex. He wanted a little thrill. But Becky had steadfastly refused to humor him.

One day, Jake brought home a gorgeous mink coat. He said, "Becky, try it on."

She wrapped herself in that beautiful garment, paraded up and down in front of the mirror, and fell in love with the coat.

"That coat," declared Jake, "costs $12,000. Do you want it?"

"Oh, do I want it!" said Becky.

"Okay, if you want it, you got to do what I want for once! We've got to have sex—just once—like the dogs do it."

Becky was taken aback, and then looked at the coat longingly. "Okay, Jake," she said. "I'll give in. Just once. But Jake, dear, not on our block!"

WHO WAS THE GREATEST golfer in the Bible?

King Solomon—he shot a thousands holes with two balls.

A SKUNK, A GIRAFFE, and a deer walked into a barroom and ordered three whiskeys. They drank them right down, and then ordered three more. The barkeep poured out the drinks, but was sort of anxious about the payment, because no money was in sight.

A minute later, they all repeated their orders, finished the drinks, and started for the door.

"Wait!" shouted the bartender. "How about paying me?"

"I can't," said the skunk, "I only have a scent."

"I can't," said the deer, "I had a buck last week, and I'm only expecting a little doe."

"Well," said the giraffe, as he turned back toward the cash register, "I guess the high balls are on me."

THE INTELLECTUAL YOUNG MAN was telling off his girl friend. "Jane," he remonstrated, "I don't think you're the girl for me. My interests are in art, in literature, and in music. You are only concerned with sports, with gambling, and with common activities that are altogether alien to me. In fact, to be blunt about it, you're downright uncouth!"

"Uncouth!" she exploded. "Me? *What are you talking about?* Uncouth? Didn't I go along with you to them operas, them concerts, them lectures, and all that sort of shit?"

Professor Michaels was conducting a class in physiology. He turned to one of his pupils and said, "Miss Jones, will you kindly tell the class what organ of the human body exudes a liquid, expands to six times its normal size, and happens to be very tender."

Miss Jones turned all colors and said, "Professor, I don't think it proper for you to ask me a question like that."

Professor Michaels turned to the class and said, "Ladies and gentlemen, this young lady has evidently not done her homework. The proper answer to the question is the eye which exudes tears, and whose pupil expands to six times its normal size. It also happens to be a very tender organ. And as for you, Miss Jones, you are suffering from delusions of grandeur."

WHAT'S THE DIFFERENCE between a sweater girl and a sewing machine?

A sewing machine has only one bobbin.

THE BRIDGE PLAYER, whose bidding had been atrocious, asked to be excused to go to the mens' room, and he left the table.

Whereupon his partner remarked, "Now, for the first time, I know what he has in his hand."

Rough Trade

A carpenter was called in to do some work in a private home. The lady of the house asked him to put up a few partitions in each large room. He did not realize he was turning the home into a whorehouse.

When the time came for the carpenter to get paid, the madam stared straight in his face and said, "Look, mister, in a business like ours, we just don't pay for anything. This is a whorehouse. If you want to take it out in trade, O.K. Just pick any girl you want; we've got twelve of them here."

The carpenter thought for a moment, realized he had been had, and then said, "Well, if that's the case, I'll accept your terms. You say I can pick anyone I want?"

"Yes," answered the madam.

"Well, I'll take you."

The madam was surprised and said, "Me? Why, there are twelve gorgeous young kids here to pick from. Why do you want an old girl like me?"

"Oh," answered the carpenter, "You're nearer my age. I'll feel more comfortable with you. Besides, you're my type. I got a yen for you."

The flattered madam consented. So they went into one of the cubicles, undressed, and started to make love.

During the process, the carpenter took his thumb and placed it up the old girl's vagina, then he slid his middle finger clear up her ass. Holding her as if she were a bowling ball, he said, "Madam, I've worked here three days now. I need the money, so let's get it straight. Either you pay me in cash right now, or I'll tear out the partition."

A TOURIST IN MARRAKESH somehow became separated from his group. While strolling in the big square, he approached a merchant who was squatting on the cobblestones, and said, "Please, sir, what time is it?"

The merchant did not rise, but simply leaned over towards his camel, lifted the camels testicles, and jogged them a bit from side to side. "It's three-fifteen," answered the merchant.

The tourist was non-plussed and amazed. Suddenly, he caught sight of his group, ran over to one of the men, and asked the time. His friend looked at his wrist watch, and said it was three-sixteen.

I'll be damned," said the first tourist. "You won't believe it, but there's an Arab over there—the man in the green striped shirt sitting over there—who can tell time by juggling his camel's balls!"

"Stop kidding me," said the other tourist.

Come over with me and I'll show you."

So they both walked over to the merchant. "Hate to bother you," said the tourist, "but could you tell us the correct time?"

"Of course," replied the merchant, and he leaned over and lifted his camel's testicles. "It's exactly nineteen minutes after three."

The second tourist looked at his watch, and exclaimed, "By George! It is! Tell me, how do you manage to tell time so accurately, by the camel's balls?"

The Arab shrugged and said, "You see, when I shift the camel's balls, I can just about see the big clock on the tower across the square."

A SELF-MADE MAN by the name of Bates managed to get his son into a posh college. At the beginning of the term, the student's family was invited to meet the dean.

Upon being presented to the guest of honor, the tycoon announced: "This is my wife, Mrs. Bates, and this is my daughter, Miss Bates, and my son, Master Bates."

"Does he?" replied the dean. "Well, we'll soon cure him of that."

Noblesse Oblige

An American had been visiting at the castle of a member of the British peerage. As was usual in such castles, the rooms were enormous, the furniture grandiose, but the plumbing facilities were pitifully meager.

One morning, the American got up, bleary-eyed, to search for the one small bathroom he was told existed on the immense floor. He finally stumbled into a room in which the duchess was taking a bath, and he encountered her Ladyship in all her nudity. With an embarrassed, "Beg pardon," the American bolted out of the room.

Fearing he might be considered less than a gentleman unless *he* reported the incident, he hastily dressed and went to his host's study, and recounted the happening in full to the duke.

The duke listened without moving a muscle. Then His Lordship remarked, "Skinny bitch, isn't she?"

The Climax of the Plot

Philippe was going on a business trip. He entrusted his lifelong friend Gaston to keep his wife out of other men's arms while he was away.

But when Philippe returned home unexpectedly, and found his dear friend Gaston and his wife *in flagrante delicto,* his rage knew no bounds. Philippe called his wife every foul name under the sun.

Then he gazed with sorrowful eyes at Gaston and said, "And you, my friend," he sobbed, "you might at least have the courtesy to stop while I'm talking to you."

WHAT'S THE DIFFERENCE between a skinny dame and a counterfeit dollar bill?

A counterfeit bill is a phony buck.

WHAT'S THE DIFFERENCE between an opera director and a baby?

A baby sucks his fingers.

A Plan Gone Awry

Jack Sanderson fell in love. Without giving the matter too much thought, he hastily entered into marriage, to his great regret.

He found his wife to be a fearful slob. She didn't make the beds; she didn't wash the dishes; she didn't sweep the floor. The home was like a pigsty.

After two weeks, unable to abide her slovenliness, he sought a friend's advice. After they had talked for hours, they concluded Sanderson didn't have enough money to get divorced, nor sufficient grounds in law for a suit.

In desperation, the despairing husband even suggested killing his wife. His friend dissuaded him, saying, "Look, you'll either wind up in the electric chair, or you'll spend the rest of your days in the penitentiary. You just can't go ahead and murder her outright. But there's no law against a man having sex with his wife as often as he wishes. Why don't you fuck her to death?"

Sanderson agreed. That was the way to do it.

During the next few days, he screwed her, and laid her, and fucked her with as much strength as he had. He only stopped when he was completely worn out.

The next day, the house was spotlessly clean. The dishes were washed, the beds were made, the place was beautiful.

Unable to understand the transformation, he asked his wife, "How come?"

"Well," she answered, "you treat me nice, so I treat you nice."

DANCING:

A vertical expression of a horizontal intention.

A CHAP WAS ROWING down the Thames one Sunday when he lost one of his oars, and he drifted out to midstream. He tried to paddle with the one that remained but found the going difficult.

Just then, he noticed a boat coming downstream, in which sat a man and two women, all three rowing.

"I say," he shouted across the water, "lend me one of your oars."

The Cockney looked up indignantly. "They're not 'ores!" he protested. "They're me mother and sister!"

Ten Bucks Is Ten Bucks

A disgruntled litigant yelled out to the judge, "Go to hell."

The incensed magistrate promptly declared, "You're in contempt of court! That's going to cost you ten dollars a word. I fine you $30!"

Considerably chastened, the litigant apologetically asked, "Your Honor, can I amend my remark to *'Fuck You']*"

ONE DAY, Mr. James Solomon bumped into Becky the whore on 23rd Street. "Gee, Becky," he said, "I haven't seen you for a dog's age. Where've you been?"

"Oh," she said, "I've been up here on 23rd Street for the last two years. You see, when my daughter Sadie got married, I gave her 14th Street for a wedding present."

The Steak au Poivre was as tough as a leather apron. The irate diner called the waiter and snarled, "I want to see the manager!"

The manager came, and politely asked, "What's the matter, Sir? Is there anything wrong?"

"Yes!" fumed the customer. "This steak is terrible. It costs $14.50 and it's as hard as nails. You can give this steak to your chef and tell him to go shove it up his ass!"

The manager left—taking the steak with him.

In two minutes, he returned, and said, "I'm dreadfully sorry, sir. You'll have to wait. The chef says that there's one *Lobster Thermidor* and one *Veal Cutlet Parmigian* ahead of you."

INSTRUCTIONS FOR USING THE LATEST DIAL TELEPHONES

On your telephone, you'll find a dial with letters to indicate the exchange you want. For instance, "S" stands for South, "P" for Pussy, and "O" for Operator. If South is required, put your finger in the "S" hole. If you're looking for Pussy, put your finger in the "P" hole.

If the Operator is wanted, put your finger in the Operator's hole, and work your finger until she comes. Then she will give you the required connection.

If you have fingered the "P" hole correctly, you'll hear a purring sound; but if you have inserted your finger in the wrong hole—the "R's" hole, for instance—you'll hear a high-pitched scream.

Where satisfactory connection proves difficult, this may be due to more than one person fingering the Operator's hole at the same time. You must then wait for service, until the other party removes his tube.

LITTLE EMILY asked her mother, "Mommy, do women come apart?"

"What a strange question!" answered Emily's mother. "What makes you ask that?"

"Well," replied Emily, "I heard Daddy say he'd like to screw the ass off the new maid."

Make Way!

In a crowded hotel elevator, one of the male passengers called out to the elevator operator, "Ballroom, please."

Whereupon the lady standing next to him declared, "Sir! I'm standing back as far as I can!"

AN OLD LADY went to her physician and complained of constipation. The doctor asked, "Do you do anything about it?"

"Of course I do, doctor. I sit on the toilet for three hours every day."

"No, no, I don't mean that, Mrs. Jones. I mean do you take anything?"

"Of course, doctor. I take along my knitting."

A YOUNG BOY AND GIRL entered the movie theater and took seats just in back of an old maid. After a few minutes, the girl began to giggle. In fact, she kept on giggling for some time.

The old maid couldn't stand it any longer. Finally, she turned to the girl and said, "Young lady, are you feeling hysterical?"

The girl giggled a little more and replied, "No, ma'am, he's feeling mine."

Paying Respects

A man visiting a bordello was warmly greeted by the proprietress. After an exchange of pleasantries, the client said, "And by the way, how is your husband Bruce?"

"Oh," she answered sadly. "He died about six months ago."

"I'm sorry to hear that," said the client. "He was one of the greatest pimps I ever met."

"Thank you," answered the madam. "Isn't that just like life. A man has to die before somebody says anything nice about him."

A YOUNG MAN eagerly purchased a book entitled "How to Hump." How disappointed he was to find that it was merely Volume 8 of the Universal Encyclopedia.

GOOD NURSE:
One who can make the patient without disturbing the bed.

THE CHAIRMAN WAS ANNOUNCING the award of the church raffle prizes. "To begin with," he declared, "Third prize, belonging to Mrs. Brandt, is a Cadillac car!" Townley, who had won second prize, became quite excited.

The chairman continued. "Second prize is this lovely cake!"

"A cake!" exclaimed Townley. "What kind of prize is that?"

"Perhaps you don't realize," admonished the chairman, "that this cake was baked by the minister's wife."

"Who cares?" shouted Townley. "Fuck the minister's wife!"

"That is *Mr. Richardson's* right," the chairman calmly replied. "He won the *first* prize!"

The archbishop was sitting in his study, figuring a crossword puzzle. His colleague asked, "How are you doing?"

"Well," answered the archbishop, "I've almost finished it, but I'm stuck with just one word. What's a four-letter word meaning 'a female' and ending in u-n-t?"

"Why," came the answer, "the word is 'aunt.'"

"Oh yes, that's right!" replied the archbishop, "Lend me your eraser."

The economic recession had got him down. He turned to his wife and said, "You know, if you would learn how to cook, we could do without the maid."

"Yes," she retorted, "and if you would learn how to fuck, we could do without the chauffeur."

A CHINESE WENT to a broker's office with a certified check for $100,000 in his pocket. He told the stockbroker to invest the money for him in the stock market. "You choose any stock you wish. I trust you," said the Oriental. He received a receipt for his money. In two weeks, the Chinese came back to ask his financial counselor how things were going.

"Ah," said the other, "I'm sorry to say that the condition of the market during the past two weeks has been rather soft. As a matter of fact, due to fluctuation in the overseas money market, your stocks have receded somewhat. I must ask you to give me $5,000 more to cover your shrunken investment."

The Chinese answered, "Okay. I send you check for $5,000 tomorrow morning."

Another three weeks passed, and the Chinese came in again. "Tell me, how things?" he asked.

"A bit disturbing," answered the stockbroker. "Due to severe fluctuations, the market has plummeted again. I'm afraid we'll need another $15,000 to cover your investment."

And the Chinese plunked down another fifteen grand.

One month later, the investor came in to see his broker. When the broker saw him, woe spread across his face. The Chinaman took one look and understood.

"Flucked again?" he asked.

Now Say Cheesecake

Sam Silverman had worked for most of his life in a Seventh Avenue sweatshop. During every February, when the days were wan and chilly, the members of Sam's union took a three-week vacation without pay, and went down to Miami.

They would come home with glowing stories. Sam dreamed of the day when he could afford to take such a marvelous trip to avoid the winter's cold.

In five years, Sam had saved up enough money to request an unpaid vacation. His request was granted. He flew down to Miami, registered in a small hotel, and stepped out into the full glare of Collins Avenue for a stroll. Then he sat down on one of the benches, to admire the beautiful palm trees. Within minutes, a woman sat down right beside him. She opened with a few questions, a conversation ensued, and the two soon became real chummy. Within an hour, they were in Sam's room, and they didn't emerge —neither of them—for three days.

Sam had the most wonderful time of his life. He came home ecstatic. Now he didn't mind his work, he was so full of memories of that marvelous vacation in Miami.

About four weeks later, a man called at the sweatshop and asked for Sam Silverman. The man was dressed in a dark gray suit, carried a briefcase, and had a business air about him. When Sam was pointed out, the man went straight to him, and said, "Are you Mr. Silverman?"

Sam said, "Yes, I'm Silverman."

"Well," said the man, looking him straight up and down, "I've got something I'd like to show you." He opened his briefcase, and spread on Sam's table six photographs which revealed Sam in the most compromising positions. Nude, Sam was rolling in bed with his lady-love, in that hotel room in Miami.

Sam looked at the pictures a moment, and then his face broke into a beautiful smile. "Mister," he said, "I'll take two of these, three of that, one of those, and four of this one!"

EVER HEAR ABOUT the tight-skinned giraffe?

Every time he winks his eye he dislocates his asshole.

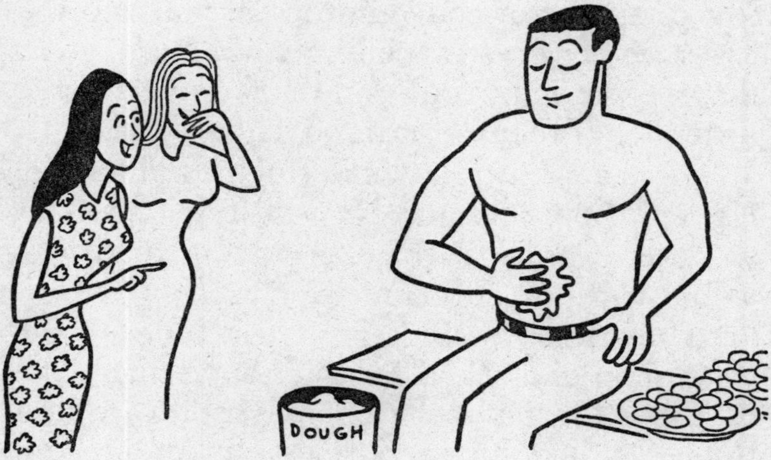

THE WIVES OF THE Army brass, along with a lieutenant assigned to them, were making an inspection tour of the camp. They wandered into the commissary where they found a man sitting bare to the waist, pressing pieces of dough on his navel. The wife of the colonel, somewhat astounded, asked, "What's that man doing?"

"Oh!" answered the lieutenant, "He's making cookies."

"Cookies!" she said, and she burst out laughing. The other ladies were also convulsed.

"If you think that's funny," offered the lieutenant, "you should have been here yesterday and seen this guy make doughnuts."

A GIRL WHO WAS about to become a bride was in great consternation. She came to her mother and said, "Look, ma, I'm going to be married tomorrow and Jack thinks I'm a virgin. I might as well tell you, I lost my virginity some time ago, and Jack is going to find this out tomorrow night. Heaven knows how he'll react."

Her mother replied, "Sally, take it easy! I had the same problem when I married your father, but I found the solution, and you can, too. You go to the ten-cent store, and buy one of those little black leather pocketbooks, that has a metal ball snap on it. When you go to bed with Jack, place the pocketbook underneath you, somewhere below your buttocks, and keep one hand on it. When Jack enters you, simply snap the pocketbook closed. When he hears it, he'll ask what that strange sound was, and you tell him that was your maidenhead that just broke."

The next night, the girl did exactly as Mother told her. During the sex act, her newlywed husband suddenly said, "Sally, what's that noise?"

She said, demurely, "Jack, that was my maidenhead."

Whereupon Jack yelled, "Well, for God's sake, open it up. You've got my balls caught!"

WHAT'S THE BEST WAY to make a bull sweat?

Give him a tight jersey.

The Entertainer

Mr. and Mrs. Robinson were dying to get out of the house and take in a show. But they couldn't secure a sitter. After much talking, they decided to take a chance and ask their next door neighbor, Fink, if he'd come in and watch their four-year-old daughter for a few hours.

Fink agreed, but he found the little girl very trying. She asked for this, and she asked for that, and she asked a thousand questions that gave him no rest and took him away from reading his novel.

When the Robinsons came home, to their utter horror, they found Fink stretched out flat on the rug, his fly open, and the little girl contentedly dangling his dong to and fro. Aghast, they turned on Fink and said, "You bastard pervert! What the hell are you doing?"

"What am I doing?" answered Fink. "I'm keeping her amused."

"Amused! Is that what you give a little girl to play with?"

"What *should* I give her to play with?" retorted Fink. "A knife?"

WHAT'S THE DIFFERENCE between a eunuch and an Eskimo?

A eunuch is a massive vassal with a passive tassel, while an Eskimo is a rigid midget with a frigid digit.

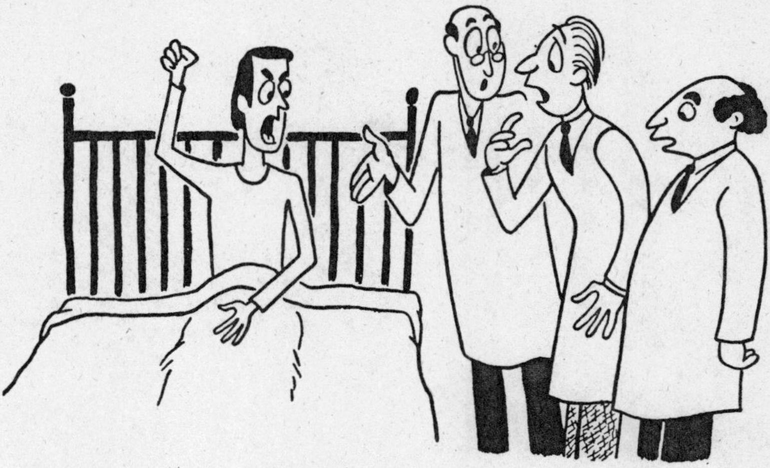

A MAN LAY IN BED in a hospital ward. Three doctors approached him and asked him what he was in the hospital for. The patient replied that he wanted to be castrated. The doctors looked at him askance, and said in unison, "What!"

He repeated: "Yes, I want to be castrated."

The operation was performed. After a few days, the patient was dressed and on his way out of the hospital when he passed the maternity ward, and saw a small crowd gathered in a room. He asked the nurse what was going on. "Oh," she said, "A little baby boy is being circumcised."

"Circumcised!" he exclaimed,"Damn it! That's the word I meant."

WHAT DO YOU CALL an uncircumcised Jewish baby?

A girl.

"STEP RIGHT UP, ladies and gentlemen," cried the circus barker, "and buy your tickets for the big show. Inside, you'll see the great Australian mountain goat, who jumps from precipice to precipice, and back to piss again.

"Also the wondrous African laughing hyena. He eats only once a month, moves his bowels only once every six months, and mates only once a year. I don't know what the hell *he's* got to laugh about.

"And then, there's the great spotted leopard! He's got 365 spots—one for every day of the year."

"Ah, sir!" asked an incredulous lady. "How about leap year?"

"Leap year? Just lift up the leopard's tail, lady."

DID YOU HEAR ABOUT the ruptured Chinaman?
He was called Wun Hong Lo.

HIPPIE: Have you ever been picked up by the fuzz?
FLOWER CHICK: No, but I bet it hurts like crazy.

A MIDDLE-AGED MAN went to a middle-aged singles dance. After he had been standing alone for a half-hour, a woman approached him and said, "Would you like to dance?"

"A Fred Astaire I'm not," he answered, "but a little bit of dancing I'd like." So off they trotted to the dance floor.

After 20 minutes or so she said, "Would you care to have a drink?"

"A big-shot drinker I'm not," he said, "but one drink couldn't hurt." So off they went to the bar.

After half an hour's conversation, she said, "How about coming to my place?"

"A Romeo I'm not," he replied, "but a little romance can't hurt," so they left together.

The next morning, as he was about to leave, she said, "How about a little money?"

"A gigolo I'm not," he replied, "but a little money I'll take."

Comeback Attempt

A down-and-out actress appeared at an agent's office and said, "Look, Tom, I got a brand new act—something new!"

"New?" he said, eyeing the blowsy dame in front of him. "Waddaya mean new?"

"Just watch." She took off her skirt, and then her panties. Then she bounced a golf ball and caught it in her twat.

"Agh," said the agent, as he turned away disgustedly, "Mamie, that's old stuff. As a matter of fact, Liz Tomaston did that trick in Paris all last summer with a basketball."

TWO FRENCHMEN, Pierre and Georges, were standing in neighboring urinals. Pierre unzipped his fly and exposed his penis. Georges noticed that his neighbor's dong was tattooed with the letters *S.E.* With great curiousity, he turned to Pierre and said, "That is very strange, Sir. What do those letters mean?"

"Well," answered Pierre, "those are the initials of my sweetheart. When you see my penis in this quiescent way, you see only the letters *S.E.* But when my organ is aroused, then you see the full name of my darling, *Susan Epee.*"

Georges then unzipped his fly, and extracted *his* organ. By a strange coincidence, he announced, his dick was also tattoed with the letters *S.E.!*

"Ah!" said Pierre, "You, too, have a girl with these initials?"

"Oh, no!" said Georges. "You see, when my penis is at rest, then all you see are the letters *S.E.* But when my cock comes to full power, then on it, you can read tattooed, *'Souvenir de la Legion Etrangere Francaise de l'Expedition Africaine.'*"

WHAT IS BETTER than honor?

In 'er!

Standing Room Only

A man entered a crowded bus with his six children. Only six seats were vacant, and each of the children ran to a seat. The man was left standing.

"Ah!" chuckled the conductor, "It looks like you've screwed yourself out of a seat!"

AFTER HAVING AN AFFAIR with a Chinese girl, a white man discovered, to his horror, that his organ had turned black. He consulted a physician who advised that his penis would have to be amputated.

In a panic, the unfortunate fellow consulted a close friend. The friend suggested that he go see a Chinese doctor, reasoning that he would likely be more familiar with such a condition.

Accordingly, the stricken man made an appointment with the eminent Dr. Wong. After the Chinese doctor had made a careful examination, he asked the patient, "Have you consulted a white doctor?"

The man answered yes. The Chinese physician then asked, "Did doctor say necessary to cut off organ?"

"Yes," admitted the patient.

Resassuringly, the Chinese doctor concluded, "Not necessary to cut off. Wait two days. It fall off by itself."

WHATS THE DIFFERENCE between a circus and a Broadway chorus line?

A circus is an array of cunning stunts.

Geographical Estimate of Woman

FROM 14 TO 18:

She is like Africa—partly virgin and partly explored.

FROM 18 TO 24:

She is like Australia—highly developed in the built-up areas.

FROM 24 TO 30:

She is like America—highly technical and always seeking new methods.

FROM 30 TO 40:

She is like Asia—sultry, hot and mysterious.

FROM 40 TO 50:

She is like Europe—somewhat devasted but still interesting in places.

FROM 50 TO 65:

She is like Antarctica—everybody knows where it is but nobody wants to go there.

WHY IS A PASSIONATE kiss like a spider?

Both lead to the undoing of the fly.

MIDGET TO PRETTY GIRL: What do you say to a little fuck?
PRETTY GIRL: Hello, little fuck.

IRATE HOUSEWIFE: My husband can lick your husband.
SECOND HOUSEWIFE: I think he does.

MOTHER: Has the iceman come yet?
DAUGHTER: No, but he's breathing hard.

That's Easy?

A man got a job in the sales promotion department of a cola soft-drink company.

When he asked about his duties, the manager explained. "Oh! It's an easy job! All you have to do is to call on ten women buyers every day, and knock Seven-Up!"

The Vow

Tom O'Connor, Pat McCarthy, and Dennis Corcoran had been friends for many, many years. Every night they drank at the same corner saloon.

Then Dennis was taken sick. He brought his two pals together, confided that he wouldn't last very long, and said to them, "I want you to promise that every year, for the sake of old times, you'll each visit my grave and bring me a bottle of Scotch and lay it on the side in memory of the wonderful days we spent together."

The two men promised.

A year later, after Dennis had been laid to rest, on the anniversary of his funeral, the two men met at his grave. Pat took out a bottle of Scotch and lovingly placed it near the headstone. To his utter amazement, Tom unzipped his fly, took out his pecker, and pissed on the grave.

"Oh," cried Pat, taken aback, "is that the way you keep your promise to our poor departed Dennis?"

"I'm keeping my promise all right," answered the other. "I did bring him a bottle of Scotch and I gave it to him, but I didn't think he'd mind if the contents passed through my kidneys just once before I presented it to him."

"THAT REMAINS TO BE SEEN" said the elephant as he shit on the pavement.

THE PARTNERS HAD ADVERTISED for a bookkeeper. They agreed that Joe would do the interviewing. They sat expectantly outside Joe's office while Joe interviewed the first candidate. After a few minutes, Joe emerged and said: "Oh boy, is this girl a beaut! I asked her how much is two and two, and she said five. Of course she knows that two and two is four. What a sense of optimism! Imagine a bookkeeper who'll take the worst figures and turn them into the most glowing results. Boy, two and two, five, that's really something!"

The partners agreed.

After his next interview, Joe gave his report: "Well, this is also a pretty bright girl we have here. I asked her how much two and two was, and she said, 'Two and two?—that's three.' Now, that's a girl who is going to save us money."

The partners thought a moment, then one of

them said: "You know, she seems a very conservative girl. We could use a girl like her."

Joe interviewed the next woman. Excitedly, he told the partners: "I asked her how much two and two was. She said: 'two and two, why, that's four.' You know, this one's really level-headed. She doesn't say five, she doesn't say three, she says four. She's got her two feet on the ground."

A perplexed partner looked at Joe and said: "Joe, you've really got a problem here. Tell me: which one are you going to hire?"

"Ah," Joe replied, "That's easy. The one with the big tits."

ROGER HARRIMAN was out of a job. He called on a former employer whom he had served as a butler. The fellow recalled Roger's good work, and recommended that he call on a certain wealthy woman of his acquaintance. The next day, a downcast Roger was back.

"Did you get the job?" the man asked.

"No," Roger replied, "I didn't get the job."

His ex-employer wondered why.

"Well," answered Roger, "I was interviewed by that lady. She asked for my name, my age, my experience, and everything seemed to be going all right. She asked me to set a table for her, and she seemed quite satisfied. But then she asked me to show her my testimonials—and I guess that's where I made my big mistake."

THE PRAYER of a Catholic girl:

"O Virgin Mother, thou who didst conceive without sinning, teach me to sin without conceiving."

A MAN TOOK HIS SON to a specialist. The boy was afflicted with an extremely severe case of halitosis which no doctor had been able to cure or even allay.

The specialist sat the boy in a chair and said, "Open your mouth."

The boy obliged, and a blast of unbelievably foul breath knocked the doctor over.

The physician pulled himself off the floor, brushed his clothes, and addressed the boy's father. "This, indeed, is a very severe case. In fact, his breath is so bad that the condition can only be treated gradually. As a first step, during all of next week, I want him to gargle every day with shit."

ITALIAN GUIDE: We are now passing the most fabulous brothel in Rome.

MALE TOURIST: Why?

OLD ROGUE: There may be winter in my hair, but there's summer in my heart.

YOUNG DEAR: Yes, but is there any spring in your ass?

"QUICK, MABEL," cried John, "Come here in a hurry! I've just got my semi-annual hard-on!"

Mabel came running. She took one look and gave her opinion. "Too bad, John. What you mean is that you've got your annual semi-hard-on."

A Witness

A man and his wife were watching a movie. When they arose to leave, the woman suddenly exclaimed, "Gosh! My ass has fallen asleep!"

"That's ridiculous!" said her husband. "I've heard of an arm or a leg falling asleep, but never an ass."

Thereupon a man who had been seated just behind them broke in to say, "She's absolutely right, mister. Her ass did fall asleep. In fact, I heard it snoring."

A HYPOCHONDRIAC WAS DISCUSSING his troubles with a doctor. His wife sat quietly by his side.

"For instance, take the matter of making love to my wife," he said. "The first time I lay her, I'm chilled and I shiver all over. But the second time I fuck her, I feel very warm and I perspire profusely. How do you explain that?"

"Before you reply, Doctor," interrupted the wife, "you should know that the first time he lays me, it's January; and the second time, it's June."

Propriety

He was an English teacher and she was one of his pupils. It was exceedingly dark when they parked in Lover's Lane.

After a little sparring, she exclaimed, "My! It's gruesome!"

"Such grammar!" he scolded.

A YOUNG MAN ENTERED a drug store, and asked the female clerk for some prophylactics.

"What size?" she asked.

"I don't know," he replied, "I didn't even know they came in sizes."

"Well, come into the back room," she said.

He followed. She asked him to unzip his fly. Then she then took out a rubber, tried to slip it on his penis, but it wouldn't go on. She said she thought he needed a size six.

She then took the size six rubber and tried to roll it on his organ, to no avail. "No," she remarked, "I was mistaken. You need a size eight."

She then started to slide a larger rubber on his organ. By now, the young man couldn't control himself, and shot a load.

"Well," she asked, "how many will you have?"

"None right now," he replied, "I was just shopping."

A HONEYMOON COUPLE was spending their first night in bed. He grew very ardent and exclaimed rapturously in shrill tones, "I love you! I love you! I love you!"

She grew very passionate and pleaded ecstatically, "Deeper! Deeper! Oh, Jack! Deeper!"

In response, he lowered his voice to a deep basso and said, "I love you! I love you!"

A MARRIAGE BROKER was trying to promote a match for a handsome young man who was eligible in every respect except for one shortcoming: he was extremely coarse and found it difficult to refrain from using the language of the gutter.

Before bringing him to the home of the prospective fiancée, the marriage broker cautioned him: "I don't want you to say a word. Just keep perfectly quiet."

The meeting took place. The young man sat stock silent and made a favorable impression.

However, when tea was served, the maid inadvertently omitted to give the guest a spoon, with the result that he did not touch the tea while all the others were drinking. The broker ventured an innocent question. "Why don't you drink the tea?" he asked, addressing himself to his client.

Whereupon the young man replied, "What do you expect me to stir it with, my prick?"

For Peter's Sake

Thompson went to a whorehouse. He paid his $20 and got his rocks off. When he was finished, the girl said, "You know, mister, I really enjoyed that. You're the best I've had in a long time. If you want to go again, it's free."

Well, that was an offer Thompson couldn't refuse. So he worked himself up, and shot a second load.

When they had finished, the girl turned to him and said, "Mister, you're terrific! I enjoyed that so much that if you want to go again, I'll pay *you* $20."

Thompson was enormously flattered. He rested 15 minutes, but no matter how hard he coaxed his cock, it wouldn't stand up. Finally, Thompson gave up. He took his dick in his hand, looked at it reproachfully, and said, "You little son-of-a-bitch bastard. When it comes to spend a buck, you're all there; but when it comes *to make* a dollar———!"

WHAT DO THEY CALL an abortion in Prague?

A cancelled Czech.

A SALESMAN, told about a very fancy whorehouse on upper Fifth Avenue, arrived at the address, and found a private mansion. He rang the bell and was met by a maid who, without saying a word, gave him a card. The card read: "Follow all instructions. Go into the waiting room, and proceed according to the signs."

The client entered a lavishly furnished salon, in which there were two doors. On one door, a sign read: "If you are over six feet, walk in here." The other one read: "If you are under six feet, walk in here."

Being less than six feet tall, the salesman entered the second door, and came into a smaller, but equally gorgeous, room. Here, too, he found two doors. On one door, there was a sign: "For men under fifty." On the other, there was a sign: "For men over fifty."

Being under fifty, he walked through that

door, and came into another room which again contained two doors. On one there was a sign: "If your income is over $20,000 a year, walk through here." On the other door was a sign: "If your income is under $20,000 a year, walk through here."

Since his income was under $20,000 a year, he walked through the second door, and found himself on 86th Street.

A MAN WAS CAUGHT RAIDING the chicken coop of a fellow parishioner. The elder of the parish took him to task and said, "You know that when you're stealing a chicken in my coop, you are breaking one of the Lord's commandments."

"Yes," answered the other, with downcast eyes, "but I didn't want the chicken for myself. I wanted to steal it for the minister's wife."

"The minister's wife!" said the other disdainfully. "You'd lose your immortal soul for her. Fuck the minister's wife!"

"Yes," answered the miscreant, "I did that, but she wants chicken, too."

THE ATHLETIC YOUNG MAN was practicing push-ups in the park. A drunk passed by, and stopped to watch for a minute, "Shay, Bud," he slurred, "what happened to your girl?"

The Pretzel Hold

The scene was the last Olympic games. In the quarters of the American wrestling team stood John Mack, the trainer, warning his protégé, Mike "Bull" Flamm, about the forthcoming match.

"You know," Mack said, "the Soviet wrestler you're about to tackle, Ivan Katruvsky, is one of the greatest wrestlers in the world. But he really isn't as good as you are. The only thing he's got that makes him a terror is his *pretzel hold.* If he once gets a man in his pretzel hold, that man is doomed. He's used the pretzel hold on 27 competitors, and in each case, his opponent gave up within ten seconds.

"So, listen to me, Bull, you've got to be damned careful. Never let him get you in that pretzel hold. If he once clamps you in it, you're a goner!"

Bull listened carefully to Mack's instructions

on how to avoid that crippling grip of Ivan's.

For the first three minutes of the bout, neither the American nor the Russian could gain an advantage. The crowd was on edge.

Then, suddenly, pandemonium broke loose. Bull Flamm had fallen into the clutches of Ivan's pretzel hold, and was moaning in agony. Mack, the American trainer, couldn't stand it. He knew the match was lost, and he left the arena in deep gloom. Down the corridor, the echoes of Bull's anguished cries still reached him.

And then, as Mack was about to enter his quarters, he heard an enormous shout arise from the stadium, a cheer the like of which he had never heard in all his long experience. The stands were in an absolute uproar. From the shouts, Mack knew that Bull had won the match. But he couldn't understand it. What could have caused the unthinkable turnabout?

A minute later, Flamm came trotting into the American dressing room. His trainer threw his arms around him, and said, "Bull, how in hell did you ever get out of that pretzel hold?"

"Well," answered Flamm, "he twisted me into such shapes that I never felt such agony in all my life. I thought my bones were going to break. And as I was just about to faint, I saw two balls hanging in front of me. With one desperate lunge, I bit those balls. Well, Mack, you can't imagine what a man is capable of when he bites his own balls."

THREE PRIESTS went to Grand Central Station to get a train to Buffalo. The elder two appointed the youngest one to go to the counter to buy three tickets. Behind the wicket stood a gorgeously buxom young lady wearing a dress of outrageous decolleté. The young priest was visibly flustered.

Finally, he blurted out, "Please let me have three pickets for Titsburgh."

When he realized what he had said, he was mortified, and ran back to the two other priests.

The second took the money and approached the window. Here, he too encountered the same upset, but managed to say "Can I have three tickets for Pittsburgh?" And then, laying down a $50 bill, he continued, "And I'd like my change in nipples and dimes."

Realizing what he had said, he was so abashed he left the tickets on the counter, and ran back to the other two priests.

The third, the eldest, then strode up to the counter to ask for the tickets and the change. Regarding at length the female clerk dressed in such a revealing fashion, he considered it his duty to admonish her.

"Young lady," he said, "you know if you go around dressed in such a provocative manner, you will most certainly obtain your just desserts in the life to come. It is my bounden duty to tell you that when you pass to the Great Beyond, St. Finger will certainly be there pointing his peter at you . . ."

It's Only Money

Gerald Jones was ensconced on the toilet—a pay toilet. After a while, he noticed to his dismay that the supply of toilet tissues was completely exhausted.

He knocked on the partition and asked his neighbor to pass him some toilet paper.

"Out of them, here, too," replied the man.

Searching in his pockets, Jones could find nothing but his wallet, and after examining it, he found himself in another dilemma. "Say, friend," he asked, extracting a bill, "could you let me have two fives for a ten?"

AT A MEETING of a congressional committee, one of the members made a motion for an appropriation of $768,000 for a bridge to be constructed across the Orentes River.

A senior member of the committee, a man of seventy-five, objected and said, "Listen, Tom, that motion of yours is nothing more or less than outright pork barrel. There's no need to spend the taxpayers' money for some useless piece of steel to satisfy a few constituents in that backwoods county. As a matter of fact, the Orentes River—so-called—is no river at all; it's only a puny stream. Why, I could piss half way across it."

The congressman who had made the motion rose to his feet and heatedly declared, "The Representative from Illinois is out of order."

The chairman turned to deliver his ruling when the older congressman jumped to his feet and yelled, "You bet I'm out of order! If I was *in* order, I could piss *all* the way across that little creek!"

A Strict Constructionist

Arnold, nine years old, was walking up and down the halls of the school when he was met by the principal, who stopped him and demanded to know why the boy was so indecently exposed.

"Well," answered Arnold, "in class this morning, I raised my hand, and said I wanted to go to the bathroom. My teacher told me to stick it out until lunchtime."

WHY IS LOVE like toilet paper?

After you tear off the first piece, the rest comes easy.

A BLONDE WAS WALKING down Fifth Avenue. A sudden gust of wind blew her dress up over her head, and revealed all.

When she succeeded in smoothing down her skirt, she saw a guy standing in front of her guffawing like mad.

She turned on him and rapped out, "You're no gentleman!"

He promptly shot back, "And you're no blonde!"

JAKE WAS LYING IN BED with Sadie, to whom he had been married for 12 years. On this particular night, Jake felt horny. "Sadie," he said, "lift up the nightgown."

Sadie didn't answer.

Jake tried once again. "Hey, Sadie, be a good girl. Lift up the nightgown."

Sadie still didn't answer.

Jake, furious, stormed out of the room, slamming the door.

In response to his outburst, Sadie locked the door.

For half an hour, Jake walked the living room. Then he strode back to the bedroom, pushed on the door, and found it was locked. Oh! So that was the way the wind was blowing. "Sadie," he pleaded, "open the door. I'm sorry I got sore. Open the door."

Sadie didn't answer.

Now Jake thundered, "Sadie, if you don't

open the door, I swear I'll break it down!"

"You'll break it down?" replied Sadie. "Look at my athlete! A nightgown he can't lift up, and a door he'll break down!"

WHAT'S THE DIFFERENCE between a well-stacked blonde in the daytime and the same dame in the nighttime?

In the daytime she's fair and buxom.

PERFECT SECRETARY:

One who never misses a period.

TWO SCOTSMEN WERE PLAYING golf. At the fourth hole, Sandy complained, "Mac, I do not feel well. Let's go back to the clubhoose."

Mac tried to brace up his friend, and told Sandy the air would do him good. But at the fifth hole, Sandy complained again, and said, "Mac, me stomach's gang wrong."

Mac once again tried to cheer him up and said, "Just take a deep breath and you'll be all right."

"But I dinna feel richt, I'm telling ye. The fact is that at the foorth hole, I let out a fart."

"Ah," said Mac, "that can happen to any of us. Don't be alarmed."

"Ah," wailed Sandy, "but the trouble is—I followed through."

THREE MEN WHO HAD RECENTLY DIED were brought before St. Peter. "Tell me, how did you meet your death?" said St. Peter to the first.

The first man answered, "Well, I was executed for committing murder. I came home one afternoon, found my wife in a state of undress, looked around the house, found a smoldering half-smoked cigar, found a strange man's hat on the chair, accused my wife of infidelity, got a cockamamy answer from her, and then searched frantically around the apartment for her lover.

"I couldn't find him. Then, as I went to the window to cool off, I looked out, and right below the window I saw a man standing without a hat, smoking a cigar. The way he looked—so nervous, pacing up and down—made me sure he was the man. I looked around for something to throw at him. I wanted to kill him. I found nothing at hand. So in my rage, I lifted up the icebox, and threw it right out of the window. It killed him on the spot. I was adjudged guilty of murder, was executed, and so here I am."

St. Peter turned to the second and said, "Tell me, how did you happen to leave your earthly abode?"

"Well," replied the second man, "I really don't know for sure. Some six months ago, I was to meet a man on business on a certain street. I was late. When I got there, the man wasn't there. So I paced up and down nervously, looked in all directions, stamping impatiently. All of a sudden, I felt something was coming down on top of me. I looked up, and I saw an icebox within inches of my head. That's all I remember. Apparently, I was crushed to death on the street."

St. Peter then turned to the third man, and said, "Tell me, how did you get here?"

"Some months back, I had an affair with a married woman I had taken a fancy to. One afternoon, I visited her in her apartment. She told me her husband wouldn't get home until late that evening, but after we had made love, and I was sitting around smoking my cigar, he unexpectedly returned home. His wife cried out in a hoarse whisper, My god! Here comes my husband! Quick! Hide!

"Where?" I asked.

"In panic, she opened up her empty icebox, and I jumped in!"

Great Expectations

After three days in their hotel room, a pair of honeymooners finally decided to go out for an evening. Calling the front desk, the groom got the information about the movies showing in town.

"Hey, Sally," he said to his wife who was dressing, "do you want to see 'Oliver Twist'?"

The bride pleaded, "Jack, if you show me anymore tricks with that thing, I'm going home to mother!"

THREE MEN WERE ARRAIGNED before a judge. The judge pointed to the first, and said, "You, you there, what's your occupation?"

"Your Honor," the man answered, "I'm a coke-sacker."

"A coke-sacker did you say?" asked the judge incredulously.

"Yes, Your Honor, I'm a coke-sacker."

"A coke-sacker?" repeated the judge. "Well, tell me, what do you do?"

"Well," said the man, "I come from Pittsburgh. When the coal is put into the furnaces to make steel, it burns and leaves a residue. That residue is called coke. I'm the guy who takes the coke and puts it into sacks for shipment. I'm a coke-sacker."

The judge shook his head, and then turned to the second man and asked, "Say, you, what's your occupation?

"Your Honor," replied the second, "I'm a cork-soaker."

"Is that so?" said the judge, "And what do *you* do?"

"Well," he said, "in Spain, where I came from, they take the bark off a cork tree, and in order to process the cork for use, it has to be immersed in a solution for several weeks. Now I'm the guy who takes the cork and puts it into the solution to soak. Your Honor, I'm a cork-soaker."

The judge then turned to the third man and asked, "And you, what do you do?"

The third man placed his hand over his face, bent his head, and answered, "Your Honor, I'm the real McCoy."

HOW DO PORCUPINES make love?
Very carefully.

But Who Wants Him?

"No, you're not going out tonight," insisted Mrs. Levy to her daughter. "I won't let you go to an affair that winds up at three o'clock in the morning!"

"But mamma," wailed the girl, "how do you expect me to get a feller if I don't go to parties and balls?"

"Never mind," replied the mother, "you'll get a feller without balls!"

Soup Opera

A salesman told his boss he would be calling on Tuscaloosa, Alabama.

"Oh," said the boss, "I know a good hotel

there," and he gave him the name. "It's a real good hotel, but there's just one thing. If you go to the restaurant in this particular hotel and they tell you to order soup, take it."

The salesman couldn't understand the warning, and asked his boss about his own experience in that hotel when he was a salesman.

Two years earlier, the boss had gone on a selling trip, arrived in Tuscaloosa, and checked into that particular hotel. He sat down in the dining room and after looking over the menu, turned to the waiter and asked for fish. The waiter, knowing that the fish was old, cautioned the boss: "Look, Mister, don't take fish, take soup." But the diner paid no heed to what the waiter was saying, and obstinately insisted on the fish. The waiter again said, "Order the soup!" But the diner reiterated his order for fish.

Finally, the waiter shrugged and said: "Okay, I'll bring you fish."

That night, the guest became very ill, called the front desk on the phone, and said he was vomiting and required a physician.

By the time the doctor came, the poor salesman was a wreck. When he came to, there was a nurse hovering over him, giving him an enema.

"Well," said the boss, turning to his salesman, "You see, in that particular hotel, you've got to be careful. When they tell you to take soup, *take soup*—because if you don't, they'll just shove it up your ass anyway."

The Climax

Sinclair had been married for ten years and had lived nine of them in agony. He was unbelievably jealous of his coquettish wife. For years, he had suspected she was having an affair with his business partner. Finally, he could stand the tension no longer, and hired a detective to trail her.

A few days later, the detective reported to Sinclair.

"Well, did you follow them?"

"Oh, yes," said the detective, "I have the report here. Last night, she left your home about 8:30, and then she met a man on the corner of Reid Street and Montgomery Place. They strolled around for about 15 minutes. Then they got into a car, and went down to Patmore Lane. There they parked for a half hour, and he made advances to her, to which she ungrudgingly responded. Then they drove to the Franconia Hotel. I checked at the desk, and found out that they were occupying Room 311. Fortunately, Room 311 faced the street. So I climbed a tree opposite their window, peered in, and saw them both standing there completely nude, fondling each other."

"And then?" cried Mr. Sinclair. "What happened then?"

"Oh, well, then they pulled down the shade!"

"Oh!" moaned Sinclair, "What a tragedy! Always to doubt! Never to know!"

A MAN MUST HAVE no pride at all,
If he writes his name on a shithouse wall.

WHY DOES A COW have a long face?

If you had your tits pulled twice a day, and were fucked only once a year, you'd have a long face, too.

WHAT ARE THE THREE most insulting words in the world?

Is it in?

The Connoisseur

A sporting gentleman at a bar insisted that blindfolded, he could taste any liquor and identify it, and tell the name of the company that produced it.

The bartender accepted the challenge. After the gentleman was blindfolded, the barflies gathered round to witness the first test. The expert took a sip, and immediately declared: "Four Roses, put out by Frankfort Distillers."

"Right," replied the bartender. They would try again. On his next turn, the expert again took only one sip, and announced: "Canadian Club, put out by Hiram Walker."

"Right again," said the bartender. "Let's try just once more."

This time the gang thought they'd play a trick on him. Instead of whisky, the bartender filled the bottle with urine. When the expert tasted this, he remarked excitedly, "Why, this is piss!"

"Right you are!" acknowledged the bartender. "But whose?"

THE HEIGHT OF INSOLENCE: To shit on a man's doorstep and then knock and ask for toilet paper.

A Real Pussycat

A man applied to a circus for a job as a lion tamer. The circus owner said, "We have a lion tamer, and you couldn't even come close to the performance that she gives. I don't think you have a chance for a job here. Come, I'll show you."

The circus keeper led the applicant to the lion tent, in which there stood a huge cage. In the cage was an enormous lion and a lady dressed up from head to toe in a spangled suit that shone like the sun.

"Now watch," said the circus owner.

The lady cracked the whip. The lion lay down beside her. The lady then unzipped her suit and was completely nude. Then the lion extended his huge tongue and lapped at her pussy.

"Hah!" cried the circus owner. "Can you do that?"

The applicant answered, "I sure can. You just get that lion out of the cage and I'll show ya."

A SALESMAN, in a strange city, met a young woman at a bar. After a few drinks, they became chatty, and he said "How about it?"

She replied, "Well, you wouldn't enjoy it. I'm not much of a lay. I practically never get turned on; and today, I feel as responsive as an iceberg. Mister, you wouldn't like it."

He persisted. "Let's give it a chance. I won't complain."

"No!" she refused. "No!"

Then he opened his box of samples, and said, "Look, see these top-grade silk stockings? Give me half an hour, and you can have two dozen of them. What's more, I'll bet you'll enjoy it."

"Okay," she replied at last, unable to resist the finery. "If that's the way you want it."

So they went upstairs to his room, and they lay clutched naked on the bed. Despite her forewarnings, he found her absolutely delightful. She wiggled this way and that way, and contorted charmingly.

"You were wrong," he said. "I can see you're really enjoying this."

"Not much," she replied. "I'm simply trying on the stockings!"

WHO'S THE BRAVEST man in the world?

The peanut vendor—he whistles while his nuts are burning.

A COUPLE WHO LIVED IN OHIO decided to go to New York for their tenth wedding anniversary. There was no one to leave their nine-year-old son with, so they brought him along. They stopped at the St. Regis Hotel, and were given a fine room with a window facing Fifth Avenue.

The second day of their visit, the husband started to get horny. But the ever-present kid blocked any action.

In desperation, the beleagured parent hit upon a plan. "Charley," he said, "Mother and I want to talk over something very confidential. I'll tell you what, son. You stand next to the window, and look out. Now and then, a swell chap with a high hat will come walking by. For every high hat you spot, I'll give you a quarter."

The boy agreed and stationed himself next to the casement.

For five minutes, all went well. But then the St. Patrick's Day parade marched into view.

The lad peered at a sea of high hats. "Holy Gee!" the kid roared with delight. "Oh, Pop, this fuck is going to cost you plenty!"

WHAT'S THE DIFFERENCE between a bad marksman and a constipated owl?

A bad marksman shoots and shoots and never hits.

Private Parts

A man who had married an old maid for her money took his bride on a honeymoon trip. They had obtained two berths on a deluxe train going to the Rockies, and she, of course, occupied the lower.

In their private compartment, all was cozy. She went to the bathroom and filled two glasses with water. As he peered from the upper berth, he saw her take out her false teeth and put them in one of the glasses, and then take out her glass eye and put it into the other glass. He almost fainted.

Then she took off her wig, revealing a totally bald head. He gazed at his bride in horror.

Now she turned out the lights, got into her bed, and coyly said, "Well, Joe, if you'd like to come down, I've something nice for you."

"Hand it up!" he answered.

SHE SAID she wanted a cocktail—so I told her one.

DOG'S IDEA OF PARADISE:

A thousand miles of telephone poles and a belly full of piss.

A VERY WELL-DRESSED WOMAN entered a London cab. When she arrived at a certain department store, she asked the cabbie to wait for a moment; she'd be out very shortly. In fact, she had him leave the meter running.

The cabbie waited five minutes, ten minutes, and then half an hour, but the lady never reappeared.

So the cabbie got out of his cab, opened the back door, looked inside and—to his horror—discovered a big pile of freshly dropped shit on the seat.

Full of rage, he drove around to the London Constabulary, ran up to the officer at the desk, and blurted out, "And she called herself a lady, sir. Looked like a lady, too! And look what she left in my cab!"

"Don't have time for that!" answered the lieutenant impatiently. "Whatever the lady left, take it to Whitechapel, leave it there for 30 days, and then, if nobody claims it, it's yours!"

AN AMERICAN WAS TRAVELING through England by train. As the train stopped at a small station, the American, who was seated next to a window, overheard a conversation between two Englishmen standing on the platform.

"Tom, that was simply a ripping weekend at your place. I had a dashing time, and I thank you ever so much. And as for your wife, oh! she was absolutely terrific in bed."

The American couldn't believe his ears. He stared at the two men, saw them shake hands, and then watched the visitor board the train. As it happened, the man came directly into the compartment of the American and sat down beside him. The American could not contain his curiosity. "Say, weren't you the gentlemen I just saw standing on the platform, talking to a man who wore a gray-plaid suit?"

"Yes, I am," replied the Englishman. "That was my friend Jim Powers."

"But didn't I hear you say that his wife was absolutely super in bed?"

"Yes, I did. But the truth is, she isn't much at all. But Jim's such a grand person; I just couldn't bring myself to hurt his feelings."

THE SALESMAN WHO CALLED on rural areas ran into a hard time one night. The folks put him in the same bed with "Grandpa" who had a bad habit of talking in his sleep. During the night, old Grandpa was reliving his youthful days.

"Bring on the girls!" shouted Grandpa.

The salesman shook him, but Grandpa stayed asleep and again cried out, "Bring on the girls!"

Hours later, the salesman was at last about to doze off when the old boy started to cuddle up to him again. The harassed salesman couldn't take this kind of stuff; he roughed up his romantic bedmate with a few slaps to awaken him.

"Listen, Grandpa," growled the salesman, "what you have on your mind is yours, but what you have in your hand is mine!"

MEET ME IN FRONT of the pawnshop, and I'll kiss you under the balls!

AN AMERICAN WHO FANCIED HIMSELF a hunter went up to the Canadian woods to hunt bear. In the fastnesses of the forest, he chanced upon a squaw, and the two had a little party.

After a few days in the woods, the hunter came home with his trophy, a big black bear. But soon he started to experience queer feelings in his nether parts, and went to see his doctor, who informed him that he had contracted gonorrhea.

"Ah," mused the hunter, "I made one mistake. I should have shot the squaw and screwed the bear."

LENNY AND MILDRED had been having marital difficulties, so they repaired to a marriage counselor. At the session, Lenny complained that Mildred didn't prepare proper meals for him. Mildred's complaint was that Lenny hadn't been fulfilling his conjugal obligations. After much altercation, the marriage counselor straightened things out; the final verdict was that Milly was to go to cooking school, and Lenny was to sleep with Milly semi-annually.

Going down the stairs, from the office, Milly, was glowing with satisfaction. As they reached the street, however, a troubling thought struck her. She took Lenny by the hand, looked up into his eyes, and said: "Tell me, Lenny, how many times a week is semi-annually?"

The Music Lover

For years, the boys had had a poker game every Saturday night. Then, one Saturday, Mike Ginsberg said he wouldn't be able to play next Saturday because on that night the great pianist Shapiro was playing. The excuse was accepted.

Three weeks later, Ginsberg, at the close of the regular Saturday night game, said he'd be absent the following week. Asked why, he replied, "Well, Shapiro is playing that night."

The same thing happened two or three more times during the next few months, and finally one of the boys lost patience and confronted Mike. "Hey, look," he said, "since when have you become such a great music lover? Just because Shapiro is playing, does that mean that you gotta go and hear him?"

"Ah, no," rejoined Mike. "But when Shapiro's playing, that's the night I can go and screw his wife."

QUICKIE: *No sooner spread than done.*

Bad Connection

A guy with a quick temper got into a hassle with the phone operator because she couldn't seem to get him the right number. Finally, in utter exasperation, he yelled out: "You can take this phone and stick it up your ass."

The operator reported the incident to her superiors. Confronted with the company's complaint, the subscriber acknowledged that he had been somewhat unruly. But the company officials insisted that unless he apologized, they would promptly yank his phone connection.

Being quite sore at the prospect of such an indignity, the subscriber refused to make the apology. The very next day, two men from the phone company came up to his apartment to pull out the instrument.

Now when the subscriber saw how things really stood, he was aghast. He just couldn't carry on business without a phone connnection, so he decided to swallow his pride and apologize. He lifted up the receiver, got the operator whom he had insulted on the phone, and said, "Listen here, dearie. I'm terribly sorry. I know that yesterday I wasn't very nice. I told you to take my phone and stick it up your so-and-so. Well, dearie, you don't have to worry now. There are two men here to pull it out."

British Sintax

An American girl visiting England was invited to a party. While dancing with a rather stuffy Briton, her necklace became unfastened and slipped down the back of her dress. She asked the Englishman to retrieve the jewelry for her.

He was very embarrassed. Yet wishing to comply with her request, he reached cautiously down the back of her gown.

"I'm terribly sorry," he said, "but I can't seem to reach it."

"Try further down," she said.

At this point, he noticed he was being watched by everyone in the room. He whispered to the girl, "I feel a perfect ass."

"Never mind that!" she replied. "Just get the necklace."

In the Biblical Sense

A woman was competing in a $64,000 quiz program. Her subject was the Bible, and she had reached the $64,000 question. The interlocutor asked: "What were the first words Eve said to Adam?"

The contestant pondered a moment and said, "Excuse me, would you mind repeating the question?"

The master of ceremonies again said, "What were the first words Eve said to Adam?" The contestant was stymied. Finally she blurted out, "Gee, that's a hard one!"

Whereupon the quizmaster intoned: "Right for $64,000!"

DID YOU HEAR ABOUT the queer parrot?

He went for a cockatoo.

A COUPLE WALKED into a judge's chambers and requested him to perform a marriage ceremony. He looked at the license they had just obtained from the county clerk. "This license," he said, "is no good. It doesn't have the county clerk's seal on it. Take it back to him, and have him affix his seal."

The couple left the judge's chambers. When they returned, the judge again examined the license and said, "The county clerk didn't fill in the date. It reads 'the blank day of June.' Have him insert the proper date and initial it."

Again, the couple trotted back to the county clerk's office and returned with the license duly dated.

The judge now asked, "How old are you, young lady?"

"Twenty-two," she replied.

"Well," said the judge, "you look like you're under eighteen. Go back to the county clerk and bring me your birth certificate."

When this objection was overcome, the judge performed the marriage ceremony.

Suddenly, noticing a little boy who had joined the couple, the judge asked, "Who is that?"

"That's our son," answered the groom.

"Your son?" said the judge, "Do you realize that he's a technical bastard?"

"That's funny!" said the groom, "That's exactly what the county clerk said you are!"

LORD THROTTLETOWN came home unexpectedly from grouse shooting to find the duchess in bed with a neighboring member of the landed gentry. Hot with anger, Throttletown summoned his butler and demanded his pistol.

The butler dutifully obeyed, and handed the weapon to the seething duke. The duke carefully took aim at the adulterer, but the butler interrupted the shot, advising, "Do the sporting thing, my lord. Shoot him on the rise, I say."

ALOYSIUS SMITH HAD BEEN rector of the Sacred Heart Church for many years. He was prim and proper beyond words and pervasively ascetic. Imagine the surprise of everyone when the Reverend Smith suddenly announced his marriage.

He had been on his honeymoon for a week; and when he returned, everyone was consumed with curiosity. But no one would dare to ask Reverend Smith about his personal life.

However, one of the choirboys thought it only civil to enquire about Reverend Smith's vacation.

"Tell me, Reverend Smith," the boy asked, "how did you find it?"

The minister thought for a moment and then ruefully answered, "With difficulty."

As the lad looked at him blankly, the minister murmured to himself, "Who would ever think of looking under all that hair!"

SUNDAY SCHOOL TEACHER: (admonishingly) Do you know where little girls and boys go when they do bad things?
LITTLE BOY: Back of Shannon's garage.

DO SOMETHING BIG: *Fuck a giant.*

A Cautionary Tail

A dog ran across the path of an oncoming train, but he misjudged the distance. The train, racing along at a fearful clip, cut off the dog's tail.

After he licked his wounds, the dog came back onto the tracks to look for his tail. Immediately, another train sped by and decapitated him.

The moral of the story is: *Don't lose your head while looking for a piece of tail.*

A Novice

Bottomley had gone broke. He had worked hard for 20 years, and finally his business folded.

His wife, Nancy, consoled him saying, "Bill, I'll never let you down. I'll get money for you. You'll start again in another business. I'll get you money. It's no shame to work for a living, and I'm going out on the streets."

Bottomley looked at her aghast. He thought she had gone out of her mind, but after she pleaded with him, and pointed out there was no other way, he agreed.

So Nancy left the house and didn't return for three days. She came home bedraggled, and placed 28 dollar bills and a quarter into Jim's hands. He looked at the money and said, "Who the hell gave you a quarter?"

"Why," his wife answered, "every single one of them."

CONFUCIUS SAY: *Woman who cooks carrots and peas in same pot very unsanitary.*

"IF YOU WANT TO MAKE OUT in this business," said the bell captain to a neophyte bellhop, "you gotta use tact. Now this job is not just a matter of carrying bags up to a room and saying hello and goodbye—you gotta use your head. The other day, by mistake, I opened a door—it was the wrong door—and I walked into the room, and there was a lady sitting nude in the bathtub. She just got a glimpse of me, and I immediately yelled out, 'Oh, pardon me, sir, my mistake!' She thought I didn't see her and everything turned out okay."

The next day, the trainee appeared at the bell captain's desk. His eye was black, and his face looked as if it had been run under a buzzsaw.

"What the hell happened to you?" said the bell captain.

"Oh," said the trainee, "I tried some of that tact stuff. I walked into a wrong room and there was a guy fucking a girl on a couch. Wanting to make light of it, I said, 'Gentlemen, excuse me!' At that, the girl shrieked, and the guy bellowed, 'So you're calling me a fag!' and this is how I wound up!"

THE NEWLYWEDS wanted to fly United, but the hostess objected.

TWO RABBIS, WHO WERE FRIENDS, decided to go down to the lower East Side and purchase garments for the coming holiday. They agreed that the best place to go to would be the establishment of Marcus Pincus. In the store, they found two suits they liked, but were somewhat concerned about the color. They went to Pincus and said, "Look, are these suits real black? Or are they midnight blue?"

"Absolutely black!" Pincus reassured them. "These suits are through and through black—absolutely suited for a rabbi—no blue at all!"

So they paid for the suits, and went out into the sunlight and started to walk uptown.

On the way, doubts assailed one of them. He said to his companion, "I wonder if the suits he sold us are *really* black. I'm not really sure and I'm a little worried."

At that moment, two nuns were approaching. They were about half a block away. One of the rabbis said, "You know, nuns wear pure black. So let's open up this package very fast, and when they come, we'll just compare—the color of the suits with the nuns' habits. Then we'll know for sure."

As the nuns came toward them, one of the rabbis took a coat, held it up, and then walking toward the nuns said, "Sister, could you tell me what time it is?"

As she looked at her wristwatch, he quickly placed the lapel of the coat next to her shoulder to make a comparison.

When the nuns reached their convent, the Mother Superior asked them if they had anything to report.

"Oh, nothing," they said, "except that we met two men, who looked like Jews but who spoke Latin."

"Latin!" exclaimed the Mother Superior. "How do Jews come to speak Latin?"

"Well," said one, "I heard it clear as crystal. One of them exclaimed, 'Marcus pincus fuctus!'"

"THIS IS GOING to run into money!" said the monkey as he pissed into the cash register.

A TRAVELING TROUPE had reached the deep reaches of the Southland. Their repertoire was limited to Shakespeare.

That night, in a ramshackle small playhouse, the ragtag troupe presented *Othello* to the folks of that backwater town. The house was sold out.

A Negro audience had been lured to the balcony seats by the posters which proclaimed: *Come see the sensational drama of the great Moor, Othello*. What great deeds might they not expect from that great black hero!

But as the evening wore on, the audience grew restive. Few could understand any of the lines, and there was precious little action.

After he had been betrayed by Iago, Othello stormed up and down the stage, crying: "Where is that handkerchief? Where is that handkerchief?"

From the cheaper seats in the rear balcony, a

voice bellowed: "Nigger! Wipe yo' nose on yo' sleeve, and go on with the show!"

The audience howled. From that moment on, the performance was a fiasco. Interruptions were frequent, and the play was soon halted.

For the following night, *Romeo and Juliet* had been scheduled. The manager of the troupe scented trouble. What's more, he smelled rotten eggs being brought into the theatre. Fearing the worst, he summoned the sheriff, who was told all. That worthy installed himself in a center seat, in the very front row.

Some time along in the play, Juliet did away with herself. Romeo, stricken with grief, ran from one end of the stage to the other wailing: "What shall I do? What shall I do?"

Suddenly, a voice from the balcony advised: "Fuck her before she gets cold."

Pandemonium broke loose. The crowd caught the mood, and it became impossible to resume the play.

The same play was announced for the following night. But now, the Law had been alerted. When in the second act, Romeo turned to Juliet and in impassioned tones recited: "What can be sweeter than thy lips?" the big sheriff stood up, faced the audience, planted both his feet on two seats, pulled out two pistols from his holsters, pointed them at the crowd, and bellowed: "I'll shoot the first bastard who calls out CUNT!"

IT WAS THE FINAL NIGHT of the great Soviet Ballet performance in Leningrad. The house was packed. Some had come from far-off cities to view the season finale of Moscow's prima ballerina Yevna Ostrakhovna. The hall was agog with excitement.

Just before the performance, impresario Ivan Dostrovich came into the ballerina's dressing room, told her that the house was standing room only, and that this was to be the prime moment of her brilliant career.

The star, utterly exhilarated, performed magnificently, and rewarded her devotees with five different encores.

On the first encore, Yevna strode up the staircase to the first balcony, and while the violins strummed, she wafted herself from the rail directly onto the stage, and performed a *pas de deux*.

For her second encore, she ascended to the second balcony, and as the drums beat a tattoo, she jumped into space and onto the stage, where she executed a perfect *arabesque*. The crowd went wild!

For her third encore, she climbed a rope to the third balcony, using only her hands. As the drums sounded a resonant roll, she leaped onto the stage, and performed a *pas de trois!*

For her fourth encore, she was hauled in a silver basket up to the fourth balcony, whence she leaped through space onto the stage and

executed an *entrechat!* The applause was deafening.

For her fifth and final encore, as the crowd held its breath, she mounted a motor scooter which ran on a single rail. The dazzling figure was sped up to the fifth balcony! Waving her hands to the enthralled audience below, she leaped into space, and landed on the stage in a *perfect split!*

Yevna didn't move. The crowd couldn't catch its breath! The feat, performed with such incredible grace, staggered the imagination! The audience hardly had enough energy to applaud.

But after a half-minute's utter silence, the hall broke into a thunderous roar.

At last, the curtain was drawn closed in

finality. The audience departed. But Yevna remained on the stage, motionless. Her tear-stained manager appeared. Through it all, he had been rocked with emotion.

"Ivan!" cried Yevna, "Do me just one favor."

"Anything, Yevna! Anything! Tell me what you want, I'll do anything!"

Then, noticing that the ballerina remained motionless, he aked: "Yevna, are you hurt?"

"No, Ivan," she answered. "But I can't move. Just rock me a little, please, *and break the suction.*"

The Scottish Way

A Scotsman had his pleasure with a nice young thing. When he had finished, he pulled up his pants, took off his rubber prophylactic, wrung it out, and then put it back in his pocket.

The damsel was outraged. "You stingy thing," she said. "How can you do something like that?"

He replied, "I'm sorry, but it belongs to the club."

A PEDDLER WAS BROUGHT to court by a cop who found him peddling without a license. While the peddler was sitting in the courtroom waiting his turn to appear before the bench, he listened to the proceedings of other cases.

A prostitute was brought up before the judge. The judge asked her, "What do you have to say?"

"Oh," she said, "I was minding my own business. I was standing in front of an attractive store window just looking at some shoes. Along came this cop, and said I was hustling."

"Well, were you?" said the judge.

"No, not at all. I'm absolutely innocent."

"Naturally," said the judge. "Your record proves that! You've been before this court six times this year. I fine you $100 and 30 days in the cooler."

The next woman, brought up on the same charge, again offered a lame excuse; and the judge, in a fury, fined her $250, with two months in jail.

The third girl arraigned said, "Your Honor, I was caught redhanded. I was soliciting. I have nothing more to say."

"Well," said the judge, "at least you're honest about it. I'll let you off with a $25 fine, and don't let it happen again."

Then the peddler was brought before the bench. "How do you plead?" asked the judge.

"Your Honor, what shall I tell you? You're a wise judge; you see through everything. Your honor, I'm guilty. I'm a whore!"

MR. SIDNEY TIMOTHY WITHERSPOON was a weekend guest at the duke's estate. In the middle of the night, Witherspoon had to answer an urgent call of nature, but just couldn't manage to find the bathroom.

In his distress, he roamed into the conservatory, found a high jardiniere, somehow clambered aloft, and perched atop of it to relieve himself. Disturbed about what he had done, he quietly dressed, and left the mansion before dawn.

The next two days, the stench was unbearable.

On the third day after the event, Witherspoon received a telegram from the duke: "All is forgiven, but where did you hide it?"

The Harder They Come

A man walked into a brothel and asked to see the madam.

"What can I do for you?" she said.

"Well," he answered, "I'd like a girl who can do it the hard way."

The madam thought for a moment, took mental stock of her protégés, and said, "Mister, we have girls here who will do just about anything. Now, tell me—I'm sure we can satisfy you—but tell me, what's the hard way?"

"Oh!" the client answered loftily. "On credit."

Medical Treatment

A woman called up a doctor's office and said to the nurse, "I'm missing my panties. I just wonder if I left them in the dressing room."

The nurse said she'd look, but came back in a moment and said, "I'm sorry, madam, but your panties are not here."

"Oh, well then, never mind," answered the other. "I must have left them at the dentist's."

WHAT'S THE DIFFERENCE between a rooster and a shyster?

A rooster clucks defiance.

A WOMAN CAME INTOTiffany's on Fifth Avenue and picked out a gorgeous loving cup that came to a few hundred dollars. She asked the clerk whether the firm would handle the engraving. "Of course," said the clerk. "What do you want on it?"

"The initials are F U C K M E."

The clerk was aghast. "Madam," he cried, "we can't do that!"

"Oh!" she said, "then the members of the First Unitarian Church of Kennebunkport, Maine, will be very disappointed."

Hypotheses

It was a fancy cocktail party. A middle-aged man struck up an acquaintance with a very sharply dressed brunette. She seemed a bit disdainful, but nevertheless continued the conversation.

After five minutes of give and take palaver, he looked at her quizzically and said, "Let me ask you a hypothetical question. You seem to enjoy the good things in life. Now suppose I was to come to you and say, 'Look, I may not be physically appealing, but I happen to have lots of money.' Suppose I said to you, 'If you would spend tonight with me, I would give you $10,000 in the morning.' What would your answer be?"

The young woman thought for a moment and said, "Well, that would be a mighty attractive offer, more than I earn in half a year. Of course, what you would be asking would be somewhat degrading. Nevertheless, if I were to be perfectly honest about it, I think I would succumb to the temptation and agree for $10,000 in cash—assuming it was just for one night."

"Yes," answered the other, "all I meant was one night. But suppose I offered you $5,000—speaking hypothetically, of course—would your answer still be the same?"

"Yes, I think it would. That would be a mighty generous sum."

"Well," persisted the other, "suppose I said to

you, 'Look, all I want is for you to be nice to me for an hour—just one hour—and I'll give you a present of $500.' Would you accept?"

"$500 for just one hour! Yes, I'll confess I'd be weak enough to take that offer."

"Suppose I said $100 for just one half hour?"

"$100 for a half hour? I don't think I'd be sufficiently strong willed to turn that down."

"Well," prompted the other, "suppose I offered you $25?"

"Are you mad?" she replied. "What sort of a person do you think I am?"

"Oh," he said, "we settled that matter about five mintues ago. All we're haggling about now is the price."

EUROPEAN: You know, I come from the other side.

FEMALE ACQUAINTANCE: Gee, that I gotta see!

YOUNG MAN (pointing): Is that Hortense?

GIRL FRIEND: She looks relaxed to me.

KISS:

An application at headquarters for a job at the front.

WHEN MRS. SMITH DIED, she went to heaven. St. Peter came to greet her. "Come in," he said.

Mrs. Smith answered, "Look, sir, I don't want to be here alone. I want to find my husband. I can't enjoy heaven unless we're reunited."

"Fine!" said St. Peter. "What was his name?"

"Joe Smith," she replied.

"Oh my God!" exclaimed St. Peter, "There are millions of Smiths in heaven, and thousands of Joseph Smiths. It would take 10 years to locate him. Can't you tell me more about him?"

"Yes," answered the lady, "he was a very honest man, and a very mild man. His last words were, 'Annie, if you're ever unfaithful to me, I shall turn in my grave.' "

St. Peter broke out in a smile. "Oh, I know who you mean. You mean *Twirling* Joe Smith."

WHY DID SANDY MCALLEN eat beans for dinner on Saturday night?

So he could take a bubble bath on Sunday morning.

Practical Philosophy

If I take one drink, I can't feel it;
If I take two drinks, I can feel it;
If I take three drinks, anyone can feel it.

A SOLDIER ON A CRUTCH limped up to a soda fountain. The girl behind the fountain asked, "What'll you have?"

"A chocolate sundae," he said.

"Crushed nuts?" she asked.

"No!" he answered. "Just shot in the ass."

A MIDDLE-AGED COUPLE consulted a marriage counselor. After they told him about their difficulties, he advised; "Your life together is too structured. There's never any spontaneity. Make love—not by a timetable— but when you really want to."

On their second visit, the counselor asked; "Well, have you followed my advice? What happened?"

"Things are really going much better," said the couple. "We made love impulsively. The only thing is, they won't let us into Howard Johnson's any more!"

THE SCENE IS A rather well-appointed restaurant. A young lady is sitting alone at a table, and can't help but overhear a discussion among four men at the adjoining table.

The first man says, "It is spelled W-O-O-M, *woom*. That's the simplest spelling. And obviously the best."

The second one says, "I'm sorry. The spelling is W-O-O-M-B. A little strange perhaps, but definitely the correct spelling."

The third one breaks in and says, "I'm sorry, gentlemen, but you are quite stingy with your letters. The correct way to spell the word is W-O-O-O-M-M-B."

"Ridiculous!" insists the fourth. "Ridiculous, I say. In that word, there's a final R. The word is spelled W-O-M-B-R-R."

The young lady, overhearing this exchange,

stands up, walks to their table, and declares, "I'm very sorry, gentlemen. I can tell you on my authority as a librarian that the word is actually spelled W-O-M-B." And with that, she turns her back and walks out.

The four men are nonplussed for a moment. Then one says, "Do you gentlemen suppose she might be right?"

"Oh, not a chance!" replies one of the others. "A slip of a girl like that? Not a chance! I'm sure that never in her whole life did she ever hear an elephant fart!"

A MAN BROUGHT two monkeys into a taxidermist's shop.

"Would you like them mounted?" the shopkeeper asked.

"No," answered the customer, "just shaking hands."

Two salesmen found themselves in a rural district, and having no place to put up for the night, tried a farmhouse, where they were given a room.

That night, the farmer's daughter, seeking excitement, came into their room, and said she wouldn't mind having a party providing they took proper precautions.

"You wouldn't want me to have a kid, would you?" she asked.

"Of course not!" answered the two.

So she gave them each a rubber and said, "Put these on."

They did, and the three of them spent a good part of the night in fun and frolic.

About six months later, the same two salesmen met again. "Ah," one of them recalled, "what a wonderful time we had last time we were together."

"Yes," agreed the other, "but let me ask you, are you worried now about that girl having a kid?"

"No," answered the other, "I certainly don't care."

"Well, neither do I," replied the other. "So how about it," he said, unzipping his fly, "let's take these damned things off!"

Welsh rarebit:

A Cardiff virgin.

Certified Pubic Accountant

Who was the first bookkeeper?

Adam. He turned over a leaf and made an entry.

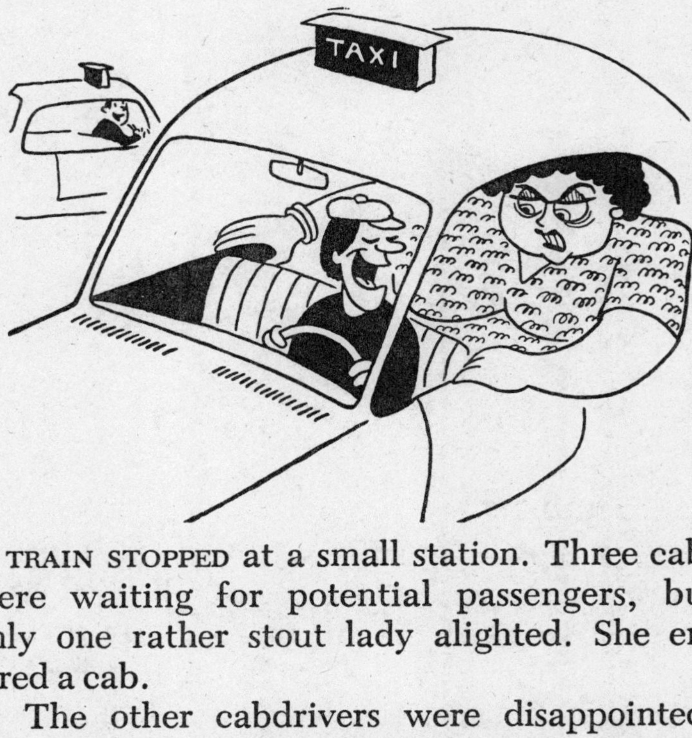

A TRAIN STOPPED at a small station. Three cabs were waiting for potential passengers, but only one rather stout lady alighted. She entered a cab.

The other cabdrivers were disappointed. One of them derisively called out to his successful competitor, "Where'd you get the fat lady Joe?"

Indignant, the cabbie shouted back, "If you don't like this fat lady, you can go kiss her fat ass!"

Then, turning to his passenger, he chortled, "That's telling 'em, fat lady, ain't it!"

WHAT IS IT that two men can do with ease, a woman and a man can do with difficulty, and two women can't do at all?

Piss in the same pot.

The Gamblers

Two hospital patients, both inveterate gamblers, were unable to secure playing cards. So they sneaked the diagnosis cards from a nurse's clipboard and started a game of draw poker. On the very first hand, they kept raising their bets until all their money was on the table.

"Well," said one, reaching out for the money, "I guess I win. I hold a full house: three appendectomies and two gall-stones."

"Just a minute!" the other spoke up, "Not so fast. I've got four enemas!"

"Okay" conceded the first. "I guess you win the pot."

JIMMY WAS TO BE MARRIED that night. Regrettably the very afternoon before the wedding, he had been in a car collision.

After an examination, the doctor informed him he would be O.K., but he had suffered a severe muscle pull and laceration in a most awkward place. It would be necessary to make a splint.

The doctor applied four small strips of narrow wood and some gauze and tape, and made a splint.

That night, when Jimmy and his new bride set foot in their bridal chamber, she started to disrobe in strip-tease fashion. When she revealed her shoulders she said, "Look, Jimmy, never been touched by any man."

Then she stipped to the waist and uncovered her boobs. "Look, Jimmy," she said, "no man's eyes have ever gazed upon these."

This routine was carried on to its expected conclusion. At last, Jimmy exclaimed, "That's nothing! Look at this," he said, revealing his dong, "mine's still in its original crate."

WHAT'S THE DIFFERENCE between frustration and utter frustration?

Frustration is the first time you find out that you can't do it the second time. Utter frustration is the second time you find out that you can't do it the first time.

STOP SCREWING AROUND—patronize your local brothel!

SIGN OVER URINAL: *Step up, it's shorter than you think.*

A MOONLIGHTER was walking home around 2:00 A.M. A streetwalker approached him and said, "Hey mister, how about a blow job?"

The man answered, "No, not for me. I got two jobs already."

One Last Fling

Three men were arraigned in an African country not exactly famed for its mercy. Since the crime they had been accused of was a sexual offense, the penalty would also be sexual. Each of the culprits was to lose his penis. Brought before the Emperor, the three were given a choice of how the penalty should be enforced.

Brought up in the land of the guillotine, the Frenchman said, "Chop it off!"

The Italian mournfully regarded his beloved salami and sighed, "Slice it off!"

The Emperor then turned to the American and questioned, "How about you?"

"I'm ready!" answered the Yank. "Jerk it off!"

"WELL, SON, DID YOU WIN the State High School Spelling Bee?"

"No, Pa, I didn't. I missed the very first word."

"You did? What was the word?"

"Posse."

"Ye gods! No wonder you missed it. You don't even know how to pronounce it!"

THE BIG SIX BAND was going great guns when someone in the audience yelled out that the piccolo player was a bastard.

The leader's baton beat a tattoo on the music-stand, and the players became silent.

"Who called my piccolo player a bastard?" the leader demanded.

A voice from the rear of the theatre shot back. "Who called that bastard a piccolo player?"

STROLLING ALONG LEXINGTON AVENUE, a man passed a shop and was attracted by an unusually fine looking antique watch in the window. As a matter of fact, there were a few hundred other watches, each of very fine quality. He entered the shop to make an inquiry. "I would like to price the third watch in the fourth row," he told the clerk. "The one that's inlaid with onyx."

"Oh," answered the shopkeeper, "I'm sorry. That watch isn't for sale."

"It isn't for sale? Well, then, why do you display it in the window?"

"The fact is," answered the shopkeeper, "we don't sell watches at all. I'm a *mohel*! You know what that means! I circumcise Jewish babies."

The customer puffed up and said, "Well, for God's sake, if that's what you do, why do you hang watches in the window?"

"Well," answered the shopkeeper, "What would you suggest we hang up for display?"

DOCTOR: (taking up his stethoscope) Big breaths.

GIRL: Yeth, and I'm not thixteen yet.

A YOUNG UNSOPHISTICATED PRIEST was walking through Times Square when a young lady approached him and asked, "Would you like a blow job? Ten dollars." The priest did not answer, but proceeded on his way.

A few blocks later, another damsel sauntered up to the priest and sweetly inquired, "How about a blow job, Father? Ten bucks." Again the priest said nothing.

When he reached his church, the priest encountered a nun and asked her, "Say, sister, what's a blow job?"

She looked him straight in the eye. "Ten dollars!" she replied.

THE PRIEST OF MY CHURCH loves his neighbor—but her husband keeps showing up at the wrong time.

Arabic Nights

Tomlin and Dinkers, both newlyweds, agreed to a bet on who could make love to his wife more times on his bridal night. They took adjoining hotel rooms. Each time one of them made love, he would carve a notch on the bedpost.

Tomlin performed at ten o'clock, and duly placed a scratch on the bedpost. Then at two A.M. he performed again, and fell into a deep sleep for the rest of the night.

At eight in the morning, Dinkers came in to examine his competitor's score.

"My god!" Dinkers exclaimed. "Eleven! The son-of-a-bitch beat me by three!"

Getting an Education

A student got married to a divorcée who had won campus renown for her amatory exploits. In sending him off on his honeymoon, his classmates kidded him on the superior knowledge of his spouse, and asked him to let them know how he was getting along.

After a few days, they received the following cable: "Flunked all tests but French."

AVOID THE DRAFT: *Zip up your fly.*

AT A LOS ANGELES PARTY, a guest boasted that he was endowed with a wondrous sense of smell. Just one sniff in the dark, and he could tell what the object was.

Following the boast, it was decided that his powers be put to the test. An assortment of twigs was brought into the room, and the self-proclaimed wizard was blindfolded.

One of the twigs was held under his nose for an instant. "Pine," said the man with the keen sense of smell. Another twig he guessed to be birch, another oak, another hickory, and so on—all correctly.

To further test the powers of the gifted nose, one of the invited company, who had just come from one of those hallway loving parties, then held his forefinger under the expert's nose.

"Hollywood," declared the wizard.

Sophistication

It was the day before the Holy Day of Atonement. A young Jewish chap in a small town had something on his conscience. He went to his synagogue to see the rabbi. In privacy, he confessed to the rabbi that he had had a sexual adventure which troubled him.

"Well," said the rabbi, "what happened?"

"Oh," answered the young chap, "I'm really ashamed to tell you. I thought you could gain me forgiveness before Yom Kippur. Of course, I'm ready to make a sizable contribution to the synagogue."

"Well," said the rabbi, "what actually happened?"

"I had sexual intercourse with a gentile female."

"That's pretty bad."

"Worse. I kissed her."

"You kissed her?"

"Yes, I kissed her in a very intimate place."

The rabbi threw up his hands in horror and said, "Sorry! There's nothing I can do for you. The transgression is outrageous. You've shamed yourself beyond repair." And the rabbi angrily dismissed him.

The young man was distraught, and drove to a larger town. He sought out the rabbi of the Conservative congregation, and told him his story. But the rabbi reproved him, though in milder tones, and advised that he couldn't accept a contribution because the sin committed was really beyond sanctioning.

The young man was crestfallen. But still determined to seek absolution, he drove to Detroit. There he sought out the largest Reform congregation, met the rabbi, and told his story.

The rabbi listened patiently and then replied, "Well, it's an indiscretion, but not a fatal error. I believe that a proper contribution to the synagogue fund, and your attendance here tomorrow at services, will clear up the matter."

The young sinner turned to the rabbi and declared, "I'll be delighted to comply with everything you mentioned. Yet, I can't understand. How is it that Rabbi Finkelstein and Rabbi Tannenbaum gave little heed to my plea and turned me out?"

"Well," answered the Reform rabbi, "do you expect such small-town rabbis to know anything about fancy fucking?"

A Measure of Luck

O'Brien, Heinz, and Cohen decided to engage in a joint venture: namely, to play the numbers game.

Each one put up a dollar. The question naturally arose which number to select.

"I have an idea," said O'Brien, "Let's measure our pricks, and we'll play the number that comes up."

They all agreed. O'Brien's tool measured six inches; Heinz's eight inches; and Cohen's two inches. So they selected the number 682.

They were lucky: that was the winning number, and they divided $1,800 among them.

Overjoyed, O'Brien remarked, "Ain't we lucky that mine measured six inches!"

Said Heinz, "It's lucky for you boys that my tool is eight inches long."

Cohen added, "You can thank your lucky stars I had a hard-on."

Sang Froid Defined

At a bar in Paris, an American was drinking with three Frenchmen. "Tell me," he asked, "what is *sang froid*? Oh, I know that if you translate it, it means *cold blood*, but I'd like to know the connotation of that particular term."

"Well," answered one Frenchman, "let me try to explain. Suppose you have left your home—presumably on a business trip—and you come home unexpectedly. You find your wife in bed with your best friend. You do not get emotional; you do not get unduly upset. You smile at both of them, and you say, 'Pardon the intrusion.' Well, that is what I would call *sang froid*."

Another of the Frenchmen standing by broke in and said, "Well, I wouldn't exactly call that *sang froid*. I think *sang froid* is just unusual tact. Suppose in the same situation you wave hello to your friend and your wife who are in bed, and with complete imperturbability you say, 'Pardon the intrusion, sir. Don't mind me. Please continue.' Well now, that's what I would call *sang froid*."

"Ah!" broke in the third, "well, maybe, but as for me, I'd go a step further in my definition. If under the same circumstances you said, 'Pardon the intrusion. Please continue!' and your best friend in bed *could* continue—well, that's what I would call *sang froid*."

PROCTOLOGIST: A super dooper pooper snooper.

A Betting Man

Joe the gambler walked into a saloon and said to the bartender, "Bet you a dollar I can bite my right eye."

The bartender said, "O.K. It's a bet." So Joe took out his glass eye and bit it. The bartender paid up, and then challenged, "Bet you a dollar you can't bite your left eye."

Joe accepted the challenge. He then removed his dental plates from his mouth, and bit his left eye. The bartender smiled and paid up.

Then Joe said, "I'll bet you a dollar I can piss on you without getting you wet." This offer was promptly accepted, and then Joe proceeded to do his thing. The bartender jumped back, drenched, and exclaimed, "What the hell are you doing?"

"Well," answered Joe ruefully, as he slapped a buck on the bar, "You can't win em all!"

WHAT'S INDECENT?

When it's in long, and it's hard, and it's deep, then it's indecent.

It Happened in a Gymnasium

The man in the shower admired the length and robustness of his neighbor's penis. "My God!" he exclaimed. "That's the longest apparatus I've ever seen. How'd you get it that way?"

"Oh," said the other, "if you want to get your dong as long as mine, do what I do. I rub it every day with butter."

The next week, the two met again in the same place. "Well," said one, "did you do what I told you to do? Did you get any results?"

"Yes," answered the other, "I did. But here it is a week later, and instead of getting longer, it's become smaller."

"But did you follow my instructions to the letter?"

"Not exactly. Butter is so damned expensive, I used Crisco."

"Crisco!" cried the other, throwing up his hands. "Crisco! My God, man, don't you know that Crisco's shortenin'?"

What's the difference between a sin and a shame?

It's a sin to put it in; it's a shame to take it out.

THE BUXOM WAITRESS asked the diners what they would like for dessert. Jake ordered chocolate pudding; Mike ordered apple pie.

"I'll take raisin pie," said Tom.

"And you?" asked the waitress, leaning way over the table towards Ronny. Ronny looked up, and after a long gaze at the waitress' very visible charms, declared, "Mine's raisin' too!"

THE AMERICAN SOLDIER stood on a London street corner.

An English lass passed by, and a gust of wind lifted her dress higher than was decent.

"A bit airy," remarked the friendly soldier.

To which the Cockney gal retorted, "' Ell yes! What did you expect —feathers?"

MOTHER'S DAY:
Nine months after Father's Day.

Aplomb

A man came into a high-toned bar and went up to the manager and said, "Look, I can play anything. Can you use a pianist?"

"Well," said the manager, "come to think of it, it might pep the place up a bit. How well do you play?"

"I can play anything," said the man. "You hum it and I'll play it."

"Well," said the manager, "there's one condition. If you work here, you've got to wear a dinner suit."

"OK," agreed the musician.

The night that he was hired, the pianist dug out his old tux and, 20 pounds heavier than when he last wore it, barely squeaked into it. His pants were much too tight, but he sauntered into the bar, sat down on the piano stool, and rattled away. He was going great guns, and the audience applauded lustily.

The pianist rose to take a bow. Just then something ripped, and the manager rushed up to the musician and exploded, "Jesus! Man! For Christ's sake, is that the best suit you've got? Do you know your balls are hanging out?"

"No," replied the eager pianist. "But you hum it and I'll play it."

A FARMER OWNED two cows, but didn't own a bull. So he arranged to borrow his neighbor's bull to service the cows.

The farmer told his son, "Go down to the barnyard. As soon as the bull is finished, come up to the house and tell me. I have to go to the cottage now, because your Aunt Matilda is visiting us today."

So the farmer returned to his house. His wife and her quite prim sister were having coffee when the boy suddenly dashed into the room, and cried, "Hey, pop, the bull just fucked the brown cow!"

Greatly embarrassed, the farmer took his son aside. "That's no way to talk in front of your aunt. Now go back to the barnyard, and after the bull services the other cow, come back and say, "Dad, the bull has *fooled* the red cow."

About 15 minutes later, the son returned and said, "The bull has fooled the red cow. He fucked the brown one again."

A TEACHER ASKED the children in her art class to depict on the blackboard their impressions of the most exciting thing they could think of.

The first little boy went to the board and drew a long jagged line. "What's that?" asked the teacher.

"Lightning," the boy replied. "Every time I see lightning I get so excited I want to yell!"

"Fine," said the teacher. "That's a very vivid picture."

The second child, a little girl, drew a wavy line with the broad side of the chalk. That was her idea of thunder she explained, which always made her feel excited. The teacher said that her picture was excellent, too.

Then little Neal stepped to the board, drew a single dot, and sat down. "What's that?" queried the teacher, a bit perplexed.

"It's a period," replied Neal.

"Well, Neal, what's so exciting about a period?"

"I don't know, teacher," the boy answered. "But my sister has missed two of them, and my whole family's excited!"

YOUNG DAUGHTER: Mommy, what's the difference between a snowman and a snowwoman?

MOTHER: Snowballs, my darling.

NEVER MAKE LOVE on an empty stomach. Feed her first.

Lovers Leap

To celebrate their 25th wedding anniversary, Mr. and Mrs. Marx went to Miami Beach, where they had spent their honeymoon 25 years back. They thought they would try to recapture the romance of their youth.

They went to the same hotel they were in years ago; they got a suite of rooms facing the beach.

"Ah!" sighed Mrs. Marx, "do you remember how we disrobed in different rooms, and then at a signal, dashed into each other's arms? Let's do it again!"

Marx agreed; he wanted to humor his wife. So they each went into a different room and undressed. At the given signal, Mr. and Mrs. Marx frantically ran toward each other. But they missed contact. Marx plunged right through the open window, and landed below on the lawn. The fall knocked him unconscious.

When he came to, he was more embarrassed than hurt. A bellhop approached him and said, "Mr. Marx, what are you doing down here? You aren't even dressed!"

Marx explained that he had accidentally fallen from his window and would like to get back to his room without being conspicuous. Would the bellhop be good enough to bring him a blanket with which to cover himself, he asked. The bellhop advised that a blanket would not be necessary; the lobby was empty.

"Empty?" cried Marx. "Where are all the people?"

"Oh!" answered the bellhop. "They're all upstairs watching the manager trying to get some woman off a doorknob she's stuck on!"

An extremely attractive stewardess on a TWA Airliner was serving lunch. As she placed a tray on a gentleman's lap, she asked, "Will you have some of our TWA coffee?"

The passenger gazed longingly at the beauty and softly replied, "No thanks. But I wouldn't mind having some of your TWA tea."

A YOUNG MAN WAS TROUBLED by a passion which he had no prospect of relieving. He repaired to a pharmacist's to get a bromide. Somewhat embarassed when he found a woman in attendance, he was about to leave when the lady behind the counter said, "Anything I can do for you?"

The young man was abashed but, after urging, finally blurted out that he had a perpetual hard-on. What could she give him for it?

"Wait a minute," said the woman, and went to the back of the store.

In a few minutes, the female pharmacist appeared. "I've just been talking it over with my sister, who is my partner," she said. "The best we can give you is the store and five hundred dollars."

FOLLINGTON, WHO REGARDED HIMSELF as an intellectual, remarked to a few of his lesser-informed friends, "If you guys will just sit down, be quiet, and afford me complete attention, I'll explain to you the theory of the atomic bomb. You see, the key is the difference between atomic fission and atomic fusion. I'll simplify the facts so that even you dolts will understand what it's all about."

"Wait a minute!" interrupted one of his friends. "Do you know why it is that although cows and goats both feed on grass, a cow craps in a big heap, while a goat craps in little pellets?"

"No," Follington replied, "I can't explain that."

"Look at him!" continued the questioner, "He's going to inform us about the atomic bomb, and he doesn't even know from shit!"

CUSTOMER: What's your ceiling price?
PROSTITUTE: Same as on the floor.

DID YOU HEAR ABOUT the queer sparrow?

He went for a woodpecker.

A YOUNG GIRL was taking the State Board examination to become a nurse. The doctor asked her, "How do you wash genitals?"

"The same way you wash Jews!" she replied.

THE GREAT FRANCOIS was entered in the annual three-mile swimming race down the Seine. An overwhelming favorite to win, he looked like a sure thing for the first ten minutes, as he splashed far ahead of his nearest competitor.

But then Francois spotted his girlfriend, Josephine. She was throwing kisses to him from the bank.

Suddenly, Francois fell behind. He seemed immobilized. His friend, Jacques, who had been following him along the shore, yelled frantically to him. "Francois, why do you not move! You are losing the race! Move! Swim! Move!"

"Ah!" yelled back Francois, "It is that lovely creature Josephine! I took one look at her, and I got so excited, it is stuck in the mud!"

"Oh!" yelled back Jacques, "Then turn over and float!"

"Not so easy!" replied Francois, "I won't be able to pass the bridge ahead!"

UPTIGHT: *Sex is great when you're up tight.*

BORIS TOMASHEFSKY was a noted figure during the heyday of the Bowery. His playhouse, situated on the Bowery, attracted theatre-goers from all over the city, and Tomashefsky was lionized.

Tomashefsky was known far and wide as an insatiable womanizer. Each night he would walk home from his theatre to his home in the neighborhood, accompanied by a different female.

One night, Tomashefsky picked up a very pretty girl, brought her to his sumptuous pad and spent the night with her.

In the morning, Tomashefsky got up, prepared a very nice breakfast, and before leaving for rehearsal, handed two tickets to his friend of the evening. "Here you are," he said. "Two seats for tonight's show. Third row, orchestra center."

The girl was enormously disappointed. She had expected a reward of a more substantial nature. She threw herself at the knees of the great man and tearfully told him that she was destitute. "Mr. Tomashefsky, I don't need tickets. What I need is bread."

"Bread?" cried Tomashefsky disdainfully, "If it's bread you want, go fuck a baker."

PRESERVE WILDLIFE: *Throw a party.*

SIX PALS WENT ON A hunting trip. One of them would have to do all the cooking. The appointed cook would stay in the cabin, handle all the chores, and, of course, be excluded from the day's fun. The arrangement would hold until someone complained about his cooking. Then the complainant would be obliged to become the cook.

There was great excitement when lots were drawn to determine just who would be saddled with the disagreeable task. Joe became the unfortunate one.

For two days, Joe fretted and sweated. On the third day, he thought he'd go berserk. The other five were out frolicking, shooting, and having fun, and he was shut up in the hot stuffy room of the little cabin. Joe decided that a desperate situation demanded a desperate remedy.

So he flung a turd into the soup and stirred it, till it was dissolved.

That night, he served brown onion soup. Sam took a spoonful. As he put it to his lips and tasted the noxious liquid, he blurted out, "My God! This tastes like shit!"

Then, suddenly realizing what the penalty would be, he added, "Tastes just like shit—*but I like it*!"

"WHY DO POLICEMEN have bigger balls than firemen?

"They sell more tickets."

THE SERVANT JAMES was sent on an errand by his mistress. It was terrifically hot, so when James spied a shady tree, he lay down under it. Soon, he was fast asleep.

A black snake in search of a good home crept up one of his trouser legs, and fell asleep too. As the afternoon wore on, James awoke with a start to find a queer-looking head sticking out of his pants. He began drawing it out, and the more he drew, the greater grew his amazement.

Finally, he addressed it: "I always knew you was black. I always knew you was long. But where did you get those baby blue eyes?"

WHAT'S MORE PROFITABLE: a one-story whorehouse or a two-story whorehouse?

A one-story whorehouse 'cause there's no fuckin' overhead.

(ON INSIDE WALL of pay toilet) SMILE, PLEASE! YOU ARE ON TV.

Say Cheesecake

The two immigrant girls entered the photographer's studio. They wanted a picture to send home to mother.

The photographer stepped behind the camera, and covered his head with a black cloth. The girls appeared frightened, but he reassured them, "Don't worry—I'm just trying to adjust the focus."

"First you take our picture," one of the girls promptly replied. "After that, you can foke us."

WHO WERE THE three most constipated men in the Bible?

The first was Cain—he wasn't able.

The second was Moses—he took two tablets.

The third was Balaam—he had trouble with his ass.

A Heart of Gold

Emma was suing a neighbor for slander. When the case came up, the judge asked her what the slander consisted of.

She replied, "The defendant told people I wasn't rich."

The judge declared, "I fail to see how that can be a reflection upon your character. Many a lovely lady isn't rich, but she can still enjoy an excellent reputation."

"That may be so," countered Emma, "but the defendant said I was pushed for cash."

WHAT'S THE DIFFERENCE between a seagull and a baby?

A seagull flits along the shore.

CENSUS TAKER: Kinfolk?
YOUNG SWEET THING: I kin folk a little.

Gentility

An American soldier was attending a swank banquet in a London Town house, given by Lady Brighton. In the midst of the gaiety, everyone felt quite embarrassed when above all the clamor, the lady loudly broke wind.

One of the Englishmen immediately rose, and declared, "Ladies and gentlemen, I beg your pardon."

Fifteen minutes later, Lady Brighton cut one again. This time a Frenchman arose and apologized.

And when half an hour later, the lady emitted a colossal fart, the one American guest arose, bowed to the Englishman and the Frenchman, and declared, "Gentlemen, this one's on me!"

RAPE IS IMPOSSIBLE because a girl can run faster with her skirt up than a man can with his pants down.

LADY:

A woman who never smokes nor drinks, and only swears when it slips out.

ONE AFTERNOON, ABOUT TWO O'CLOCK, the head of a dress manufacturing house announced to his employees that he was going home for the day.

Five minutes after he left, the employees, believing that the boss had gone to play golf and that he wouldn't phone in, decided to knock off for the day.

When Sam, the shipping clerk, came home, he found the boss in bed with his wife. He tiptoed out, and went to a movie.

A few days later, the boss again declared he was going to take the afternoon off.

Again, five minutes after he left, the employees decided to take off, and they all started to go.

But Sam kept at his work. The bookkeeper asked Sam, "What are you hanging around for? The boss has gone; he won't come back."

"I know," replied Sam, "but last time I was away from the job, last week, I almost got caught."

At a Catskill Mountain resort, a man who was on vacation without his wife and a woman who was on vacation without her husband met at table. After a couple of days of conversation, they grew sort of fond of each other and found themselves in bed together. When they both returned home to their respective homes, each was conscience-stricken. In need of relief, both confided the story to their most intimate friends.

"Well then," said the woman's confidante, after she had heard the story, "what did you do when you found yourself in this moral dilemma?"

"Oh," said the girl, "all I can tell you is that the whole week long I cried and I fucked, I fucked and I cried."

A WOMAN WAS VISITING the Bronx Zoo. Sidling up to the wire netting, she patted the kangaroo very gently. Then seized by some uncontrollable impulse, she ran her hand down the kangaroo's back, grabbed hold of its genitals, and squeezed.

The kangaroo gave one mighty leap and hopped right over the eight-foot fence and went racing across the zoo. At this point, the zoo-keeper ran up to the lady, pulled down his pants and said, "Madam, squeeze mine too. I've got to catch that son-of-a-bitch."

A YOUNG MAN who had indulged in suspicious intercourse went to his doctor and said, "Look, Doc, one of my friends picked up a gal of rather unsavory reputation, and got a little action. He says he's worried stiff. In fact, he was so upset that I decided to come over and ask you for advice as to what he should do."

"Well," answered the doctor, "unzip your fly and let me take a look at your friend."

THIS HAPPENED IN THE DAYS before the Pill. Jim, a medical student, bumped into his old neighborhood pal, Tony.

"How're things?" asked Jim.

"Not so hot," said Tony. "I've got two kids, and I'm worried about my wife getting pregnant again."

"Well," offered Jim, "there are three recognized methods of birth control. First, there's the condom, which you put over your penis, and it catches the semen. Second, there's the douche, which your wife should use to wash out the semen; and third, there's *coitus interruptus*, which means that before you come, you withdraw."

Tony thanked his friend, quite pleased that he now had the solution to his problem.

Ten years passed, before Jim bumped into Tony again. The two friends were delighted to see each other, and Tony insisted that Jim visit him and have a drink.

Then Jim asked Tony about his family. "Oh," said Tony, "I've got eight kids now, six more since I talked to you last." He then led Jim into a bedroom, where six youngsters were playing.

"Do you remember the advice you gave me? Well," continued Tony pointing, "these two are the blowouts, these two are the washouts, and these two are the pullouts."